REPORT

OF THE

INVESTIGATING COMMITTEE

OF

THE PENNSYLVANIA RAILROAD COMPANY.

Appointed by Resolution of the Stockholders

AT THE

ANNUAL MEETING HELD MARCH 10TH, 1874.

PHILADELPHIA:
ALLEN, LANE & SCOTT'S PRINTING HOUSE,
No. 233 South Fifth Street.
1874.

COMMITTEE.

WILLIAM A. STOKES, *Chairman*,
WM. H. KEMBLE,
A. LOUDON SNOWDEN,
DAVID E. SMALL,
JOHN S. IRICK,
WM. C. LONGSTRETH,
JOHN A. WRIGHT.

TO THE

STOCKHOLDERS

OF THE

PENNSYLVANIA RAILROAD COMPANY.

At the annual meeting of the stockholders, held on March 10th, 1874, the following preamble and resolutions, suggested in the report of the Board of Directors, were unanimously adopted:—

"WHEREAS, A desire has been expressed by many shareholders that a committee should be appointed by this meeting to examine all the property of the Company and prepare a full exhibit of its real value;

"AND WHEREAS, The management of the Company desire, in order to meet the views of shareholders, that a Committee of shareholders be appointed to investigate the condition of the Company in every respect; therefore be it

"1. *Resolved*, That the report of the Board of Directors, as just read, be printed in pamphlet form for the information of the shareholders, and that a committee of seven shareholders of the Company, entirely disconnected from its management and operation, be appointed by the chairman of this meeting, and by him be requested to serve as a committee to examine the report and examine into the condition of the Company; to make an appraisement of the value of the roads, shops, machinery, real estate, depots, bonds, stocks, and all other assets of the Company; also, to examine into the liabilities and obligations of the Company, including all its guarantees for other lines, with the sources of revenue to meet the same; also, its contracts and relations with other companies and parties of every kind; and to report the results of this examination to the shareholders in such form as said committee may deem most advisable for the interest and information of the shareholders, either by printed report for distribution or, at their option, by calling a meeting of the shareholders to present their report, giving thirty days' notice of such meeting by advertising in the usual form.

" 2. *Resolved*, That the president, directors, and officers of the Company be requested to furnish such committee with all needful information and facilities to enable them to accomplish the object of their appointment.

" 3. *Resolved*, That the chairman of this meeting be requested to appoint a committee of seven shareholders of this Company to recommend, after conferring with the president, a ticket for directors, to be voted by the shareholders at the next annual election—as directed by the existing resolution, adopted by the shareholders February 1st, 1858.

" 4. *Resolved*, That in the event of any of the shareholders declining or being unable to serve on either of the foregoing committees, his honor the Mayor of the city of Philadelphia, as chairman of this meeting, be authorized and requested to fill such vacancies by the appointment of other shareholders of this Company who may be in like manner entirely disconnected from its management and operation."

In pursuance of the above proceedings, his Honor William S. Stokley, Mayor of the city of Philadelphia and Chairman of the meeting, appointed the undersigned Committee of Investigation, who now respectfully present the following

REPORT.

That immediately after their appointment they met and organized by the selection of William A. Stokes as Chairman, and A. Loudon Snowden as Secretary. The necessary sub-committees were formed and the work of investigation began. We have labored diligently at the enormous mass of complicated and varied detail to ascertain the facts necessary to enable us to report correctly on the subjects involved in the resolutions, and to draw from them just conclusions as to the value of your property, the security of your investments, the guarantees and leases for which you are liable, the wisdom of the past policy of your Company, and to make any suggestions that we may deem likely to conduce to its greater prosperity in the future. To compass these points, we propose to discuss them in the following order:—

	Page
ARTICLE I.—Revision of the General Account of December 31st, 1873,	8
1. Liabilities,	9
2. Assets,	11
ARTICLE II.—Real Estate, Buildings, Machinery, Equipment, Telegraph Lines, Bridges, and Track of Road,	19
ARTICLE III.—Liabilities of the Pennsylvania Railroad Company as endorser, guarantor, lessee, or otherwise, with the result of these liabilities in 1873, and an estimate of the probable future claims on account of endorsements, &c.,	27
ARTICLE IV.—An Inquiry into the Policy, Groups, and Results of all the Railways and Canals owned or controlled by the Pennsylvania Railroad Company, subdivided thus:—	
1. Western Group, embracing the Fort Wayne or Northern System, the Pittsburg, Cincinnati and St. Louis or Southern System, the Pennsylvania Company,	46
2. Value of the competitive passenger travel and freight received from and sent to the western lines over the Pennsylvania Railroad main line,	70
3. Railroad interests south of Cairo and Baltimore,	75
4. Eastern Group, embracing the Pennsylvania System,	77

	Page
ARTICLE V.—Capital Account and Earnings of all the Railways under the control of the Pennsylvania Railroad Company, tabulated in systems, ...	113
ARTICLE VI.—Use of your Road by the Cars of Private Persons or Corporations, . . .	117
1. The Empire Transportation Company,	119
2. The Pullman Palace Car Company, .	125
ARTICLE VII.—Coal Lands, ...	129
1. Lykens Valley, ...	129
2. Shamokin Region, ...	131
3. Hazleton Property, ...	132
4. Susquehanna Coal Company, .	133
5. Policy of Owning and Working, .	136
6. Transportation of Coal, . .	138
ARTICLE VIII.—Finances, subdivided thus:—	
1. Mode of control of other roads, .	141
2. The necessity for the Pennsylvania Railroad Company managing the finances of roads under its control, .	143
3. Floating Debt, ...	145
4. Construction Account, . . .	146
5. Reduction of Capital Stock and Funded Debt, ...	147
6. Funded Debt, ...	148
7. Future Profits of the Company, .	153
8. Summary of Present and Future Financial Wants, ...	155
ARTICLE IX.—In regard to the Election of Directors by Directors, and the Acceptance of Laws without the sanction of the Stockholders, ...	158
ARTICLE X.—The sources of Existing Distrust in the Value of Railway Stocks and Securities, ...	159

	Page
ARTICLE XI.—Organization,	165
ARTICLE XII.—*Résumé*,	181
ARTICLE XIII.—Conclusion,	187
ARTICLE XIV.—Resolutions,	190
APPENDIX A.—Statements of Capital Stock and Bonds held by the Pennsylvania Railroad Company, and valuation of same; also, Statement of Capital and Operations of all Roads owned and controlled,	196
APPENDIX B.—Comparative Statement of Earnings and Expenses of Leased Lines of Pennsylvania Company (including Indianapolis and Vincennes Railroad) for six months ending June 30th, 1874, and June 30th, 1873,	219
APPENDIX C.—Comparative Statement of Earnings and Expenses of Pennsylvania Railroad and Branches and United Railroads of New Jersey for the six months of 1873 and 1874,	223
APPENDIX D.—Statement of Gross Earnings, Number of Tons of Freight moved, and Number of Passengers Carried on Lines Operated or otherwise Controlled by the Pennsylvania Company for 1873, as compared with 1868,	224
APPENDIX E.—Statement of Bonds of the several Companies, with the Time of Maturity, in chronological order,	232
APPENDIX F.—Map of Pennsylvania and New Jersey Railroads and Branches,	241
APPENDIX G.—General Map of Railroads, showing the connections of the Pennsylvania Railroad and the Pennsylvania Company,	242

ARTICLE I.

Revision of the General Account of December 31st, 1873.

To arrive at a correct knowledge of the present financial condition and value of the real and personal property of the Pennsylvania Railroad Company, we have found it necessary to depart somewhat from the general system of accounts, and divide the liabilities and assets into classes—

1. Liabilities.

These may be divided into two classes, viz., direct and contingent. The direct liabilities may again be subdivided into three kinds—first, liabilities to the bondholders; second, liabilities to the floating debt and other creditors; and, third, liabilities to the stockholders. The contingent liabilities may be subdivided into two classes—first, those from which no profit can be derived, but a failure on the part of the principals to meet which may incur loss to the guarantors. Under this head come bonds issued and secured by mortgage upon the property of other companies, and which bear the endorsement of the Pennsylvania Railroad Company; and, second, the yearly liabilities as lessee or guarantor from which the Company expects to derive a direct profit. These consist of leases made directly to the Pennsylvania Railroad Company, and to other companies in conjunction with your Company, and for which your Company is liable to pay an annual fixed rental.

2. Assets.

These consist of—

1. *Actual Assets.*—Consisting of the road, equipment, real estate, and telegraph line of your Company, the bonds and

stocks of other corporations, and the debts due by individuals and corporations.

2. *Apparent Assets.*—Of intrinsic value in themselves, being the difference in value of the real estate and equipment of the road as charged upon the books of the Company at the time of purchase and its present market value. These assets are the real basis upon which the Company is enabled to earn such large dividends upon its stock.

3. *Prospective Assets.*—Being the future profits expected to be realized upon leased roads and property.

Liabilities.

Your committee have given the general account of the treasurer, accompanying the annual report, a careful and most rigid investigation. The direct liabilities, as shown by the debtor side of the general account, are correct, being copied from the accounts in the general ledger; but large sums having been charged off from the creditor side of this account by your committee, as hereafter explained, the balance to the credit of profit and loss has been reduced to $4,985,254.46, the contingent fund being a mythical account, and really belonging to profit and loss. The reasons for these reduced valuations will be found in an itemized statement in the discussion of our assets. The item of "appraised value of securities owned by the United New Jersey Railroad and Canal Company," amounting to $4,322,225.25, as it appears on both sides of the general account, has been stricken from our statement, as it forms no part of the assets or liabilities of the Pennsylvania Railroad Company, but is a part of the property leased by the United Companies of New Jersey, and is already represented in the capital stock of those companies, and whatever income accrues therefrom goes into the treasury of the Pennsylvania Railroad Company as a part of the profit derived from operating the New Jersey lines.

The debtor side of the general account will then stand as follows:—

Dr.	REVISED GENERAL ACCOUNT.		
To capital stock, full paid,		$67,056,750 00	
Part paid,		1,087,725 00	
Total amount of capital paid in,			$68,144,475 00
To first mortgage bonds due 1880,		$4,970,000 00	
" second " " " 1875,		4,865,840 00	
" general " " " 1910,		19,558,760 00	
" consol'd " " " 1905,		8,245,000 00	
" Lien of the State upon the public works between Philadelphia and Pittsburg, bearing five per cent. interest, payable in annual installments of $460,000, applicable first to the interest, and the remainder to principal, the original amount of which was $7,500,000,		5,401,675 41	
" Mortgages and ground-rents at six per cent. remaining on real estate purchased,		104,509 32	
			43,145,784 73
" Bills payable,		$2,470,963 90	
" Acceptances given to other companies,		2,140,833 34	
			4,611,797 24
" Accounts payable, including freight and passenger balances due to other roads, pay-rolls and vouchers for December, 1873, paid in January, 1874; also, dividends unpaid and dividend scrip outstanding,			11,658,791 12
" Balance to credit of profit and loss,			4,985,254 46
			$132,545,102 55

NOTE.—The item of acceptances given for the benefit of other companies, amounting to $2,140,833.34, has been, since the date of the report, paid by the companies for whom the acceptances were made, and a very large proportion of the amounts included under the heading of accounts payable, including freight and passenger balances due to other companies, &c., and amounting to $11,658,791.12, are simply moneys due to railroad companies for balances as above stated, while an almost similar amount is due from these companies to the Pennsylvania Railroad Company under some other head; so that really your indebtedness beyond the bonded debt, instead of being $16,270,588.36, did not exceed $12,000,000. We refer you to a succeeding article discussing in detail the contingent liabilities of the Company as endorser or guarantor.

ASSETS.—*Actual Assets.*

The credit side of general account, as revised by the committee, stands as follows:—

REVISED GENERAL ACCOUNT.		CR.
By balance standing on books of the Company for the construction of the railroad between Harrisburg and Pittsburg, including the branches to Indiana and Hollidaysburg (in all two hundred and seventy-six miles); also, for the cost of stations, warehouses, shops, and shop machinery, on the whole road from Philadelphia to Pittsburg,	$19,610,223 81	
" Balance standing on the books of the Company for the purchase of the Philadelphia and Columbia Railroad,	5,375,733 43	
" Balance standing to debit of equipment of road, consisting of eight hundred and seventy-eight locomotives, three hundred and eighty-five passenger cars, one hundred and thirty-six baggage, mail, and express cars, sixteen thousand two hundred and eighty-two freight cars, and one thousand three hundred and seven road cars,	15,333,714 44	
" Cost of real estate of Company and telegraph line,	6,563,618 68	
" Extension of Pennsylvania Railroad to the Delaware river, including wharves and grain elevator,	1,688,517 82	
Total amount charged to construction, equipment, and real estate accounts for the railroad between Philadelphia and Pittsburg, comprising nine hundred and ninety-four miles of single track, including sidings, stations, warehouses, shops,		$48,571,808 18
OTHER ASSETS.		
By amount of bonds of railroads and other corporations,	$22,045,575 00	
" Amount of capital stock of railroads and other corporations,	27,665,512 00	
Total value of bonds and stocks belonging to the Company,		49,711,087 00
" Amount of fuel and materials on hand for repairs to locomotives, cars, and maintenance of way, for the Pennsylvania Railroad, United New Jersey Railroad and Canal, and the Philadelphia and Erie Railroad,		4,945,650 67
" Amount of bills and accounts receivable and amounts due from other companies, including amounts due from the Philadelphia and Erie Railroad Company, and from the United New Jersey Railroad and Canal Companies for permanent improvements, as well as for expenditures on the Harsimus Cove property at Jersey City; also, for purchase of anthracite coal properties and advances made to railroad corporations, including purchases of equipment in use on some of these lines,		23,945,107 44
" Appraised value of suspense account,		1,000,000 00
" Balance in hands of agents,		2,058,862 05
" Balance in hands of treasurer,		2,312,587 21
		$132,545,102 55

The alterations and reductions made from the statements of the stocks and bonds owned by the Company December 31st, 1873, can be best understood by an examination of the tables in the Appendix A, which exhibit in detail all the facts and figures and the basis of the valuation of each item, and it should be borne in mind that this valuation is made at a time of great financial depression.

It will be noted that the road, equipment, real estate, and telegraph lines are stated in this account as they stand charged on the books of the Company, while the value of the other assets stand as estimated by the committee, who, in valuing these securities, have adopted various rules—the three most important of which are, *first*, to take their cash market value; *second*, as to such as have not a market value commensurate with their true worth we have made careful inquiries and placed them at their intrinsic worth; and *third*, such as have neither a market nor an intrinsic value have been estimated at such price as their voting power gives to the Company. The result of this appraisement is, that while in some instances we have increased the valuation, in others we have reduced the values, showing a final result of reduced valuation on the stocks, &c. below the cost as charged on the books of the Company:—On the stocks held by the Company, $2,618,608.86; on the bonds, $362,723.23; and on the bills receivable and book debts, $2,033,979.70; and we have increased the credits by placing a valuation upon suspense account of $1,000,000; and also increased the valuation of fuel and materials on hand $157,002.82, being certain material found on leased roads that were overlooked when the inventories were taken. A very large part of the reduction in the valuation of stock is made in the stock of four roads, viz., the Allegheny Valley, Philadelphia and Erie, Pittsburg, Cincinnati and St. Louis, and the Baltimore and Potomac Railroads.

The forty-one thousand five hundred shares of stock of the Allegheny Valley Railroad Company were valued on December 31st, 1873, by the treasurer of your Company, at cost, $1,100,000; but in consequence of the financial difficulties which that company has met with since that date, this stock has now no market value; but we think it is worth to your Company, for the control it gives you of that line, and its future possibilities, at least ten dollars per share, making a change thereby of $685,000 in the valuation of that stock.

Of the Philadelphia and Erie Railroad stock you hold thirty-one thousand six hundred and thirty-six shares of the common stock, costing $779,637 26
And forty-eight thousand shares of the preferred special stock, costing . . . 1,680,000 00

The whole amounting to $2,459,637 26

We regret to express our opinion that this road is worth but little more than its bonded debt; that its floating debt can therefore have but a nominal value, which renders the common stock worthless and the preferred stock dependent altogether on future increase of trade. We have therefore made no valuation of the common stock, and have valued the preferred stock at $10 per share, on the basis of the value of the control of this road to your other interests and its possible future. This will reduce the above amount of $2,459,637.26 to $480,000, and show a loss of $1,979,637.26.

The large sum of $2,250,000—the cost of sixty thousand shares of second preferred stock of the Pittsburg, Cincinnati and St. Louis Railway Company—we charge off, and estimate as lost, because the first mortgage consolidated bonds of this company are now selling at sixty-five per cent.; the second mortgage (of $5,000,000) and the first preferred stock have no market value; the second preferred stock, which is held by the Pennsylvania Railroad Company, cannot, therefore, be now estimated at any price,—its value, like the stocks already named, will depend entirely on the future large increase of the trade on this road and its leased lines.

Of the Baltimore and Potomac Railroad stock the Pennsylvania Railroad Company holds thirty-six thousand five hundred and seventy-two shares, which cost $876,880, which we placed at the nominal value of $1 per share. When we state that the entire receipts of this road in 1873 were but $381,536.73, and its net earnings $69.93, we think we have demonstrated that the most that can be expected of it will be, that it will be able to take care of the interest on its $4,500,000 mortgage bonds, amounting to $270,000 in gold per annum.

The entire business of the Baltimore and Ohio Railroad, between Baltimore and Washington, for any one year since the termination of the war, has not reached $500,000. The most sanguine can, therefore, expect no more from this road than that it may not prove a charge to the endorsers on its bonds, viz., the Pennsylvania and the Northern Central Railroad Companies.

Book Debts.

The large reduction in the valuation of the book debts is due to the fact that the managers, in making up their December accounts, estimated as good a number of accounts which are now worthless. Of these, amounting to $2,033,979.70, there is due by the Baltimore and Potomac Railroad $1,756,703.66.

It will be observed that most of the losses above enumerated have occurred from one of two causes, both of which we utterly condemn—first, in the case of the Philadelphia and Erie, by the Pennsylvania Railroad Company occupying the double position of landlord and tenant,—of landlord, in holding so large a line of the stock of the company, and of tenant, in advancing funds to the landlord without sufficient security; and second, in making investments south of Baltimore without your consent, by which nearly $5,000,000 have been lost to your Company. We say without your consent, for we feel assured that no general resolution ever passed by you was intended to convey to the former managers of your road the power to invest nearly $10,000,000 for the acquisition of $400,000 of annual receipts, and that, too, at an expense equal to those receipts. This large expenditure of money illustrates the dangers against which we endeavor to guard, as explained in other parts of this report.

Your committee confess that they have strong hopes of some future value in the large amount charged off to profit and loss, but as we are rendering you an account of the present value of your property, we prefer to err on the side of prudence, and whatever disappointment you may meet with will be on the right side.

It will be observed that the report of the President for 1873 shows a net profit for the year of $1,513,077.44, whilst the profit and loss account is decreased $76,591. This apparent inconsistency arises from the fact that of the losses in Southern and other investments, amounting to $3,117,779.45, there was charged to profit and loss $1,589,668.44 and the balance to the securities then on hand, they having appreciated to fully that amount at that time.

For itemized value of real estate, buildings, machinery, rolling stock, track of road, &c., we refer you to a separate article, showing the value of these items to be $94,398,483.80.

We here place before you the general account, as revised by your committee, with the figures on the credit side changed to show our valuation of all the items:—

Dr.	REVISED GENERAL ACCOUNT.		
To capital stock,	full paid, $67,056,750 00		
	Part paid, 1,087,725 00		
	Total amount of capital paid in,		$68,144,475 00
To first mortgage bonds due 1880,	$4,970,000 00		
" second " " " 1875,	4,865,840 00		
" general " " " 1910,	19,558,760 00		
" consol'd " " " 1905,	8,245,000 00		
" Liens of the State upon the public works between Philadelphia and Pittsburg, bearing five per cent. interest, payable in annual installments of $460,000, applicable first to the interest and the remainder to principal, the original amount of which was $7,500,000,	5,401,675 41		
" Mortgages and ground-rents at six per cent. remaining on real estate purchased,	104,509 32		
			43,145,784 73
" Bills payable,	$2,470,963 90		
" Acceptances given to other companies,	2,140,833 34		
			4,611,797 24
" Accounts payable, including freight and passenger balances due to other roads, pay-rolls and vouchers for December, 1873, paid in January, 1874; also, dividends unpaid and dividend scrip outstanding,			11,658,791 12
" Balance to credit of profit and loss,			50,810,930 08
			$178,371,778 17

	REVISED GENERAL ACCOUNT.		Cr.
By road-bed and track and bridges,		$45,164,223 00	
" Real estate and buildings,		27,865,240 00	
" Machinery and tools,		1,270,420 00	
" Rolling stock,		20,098,600 80	$94,398,483 80
" Amount of bonds of railroads and other corporations,	$22,045,575 00		
" Amount of capital stock of railroads and other corporations,	27,665,512 00		
Total value of bonds and stock belonging to the Company,			49,711,087 00
Amount of fuel and material on hand for repairs to locomotives, cars, and maintenance of way for the Pennsylvania Railroad, United New Jersey Railroad and Canal, and the Philadelphia and Erie Railroad,			4,945,650 67
Amount of bills and accounts receivable and amount due from other roads, including amount due from the Philadelphia and Erie Railroad Company and from the United New Jersey Railroad and Canal Companies for permanent improvements, as well as for expenditures on the Harsimus Cove property at Jersey City; also, for purchase of anthracite coal properties and advances made to railroad corporations, including purchase of equipment in use on some of these lines,			23,945,107 44
" Appraised value of suspense account,			1,000,000 00
" Balance in hands of agents,			2,058,862 05
" Balance in hands of treasurer,			2,312,587 21
			$178,371,778 17

The above account shows total assets of the
Company amounting to $178,371,778 17
The bonded debt and all other liabilities
other than to stockholders, . . . 59,416,373 09
                                              $118,955,405 08
The amount of capital stock issued, . . 68,144,475 00

Leaving surplus value to credit of profit
and loss, ... $50,810,930 08

Which will make each share of the one million three hundred and sixty-three thousand shares of the stock of the

Company represent a value of $87.28, or $37.28 beyond its par value.

As to the ability of the Company to earn dividends, the first half of the present year shows net earnings on those roads directly affecting your treasury, viz., the Main Line and United Roads of New Jersey, as compared with 1873, as follows:—

Net Earnings.

United Roads, 1874,		$1,147,057 74
Main Line, 1874,		4,329,577 54
Total,		$5,476,635 28
United Roads, 1873,	$516,666 39	
Main Line, 1873,	3,895,294 88	
		4,411,961 27
Increase of net earnings in 1874,		$1,064,674 01

The leased roads demonstrate improvement, as is shown elsewhere in this report. There can be no doubt of the ability of the Company to earn, not only its usual ten per cent. dividend, but a surplus over and above all expenses, liabilities, and contingencies.

ARTICLE II.

Real Estate, Buildings, Machinery, Equipment, Telegraph Lines, Bridges, and Track of Road.

1. Land and Buildings.

Railroads are generally restrained, at their commencement, not only by want of pecuniary means, but by efforts to bring the cost of construction within the engineers' estimates. Consequently, as little land as possible is taken for stations, depots, and workshops. It follows that when the line goes into operation the quantity of land for these purposes is found to be inadequate, and this deficiency becomes greater in proportion to the success of the road. It is then necessary to purchase other property at greatly increased cost—this increase being caused by the operations of the road, so that the company is made to pay for the enhanced values of its own creation.

The far-seeing wisdom of the managers of the Pennsylvania Railroad anticipated much of this, and their far-reaching action, in a great measure, guarded against such costly consequences. At almost every point, and especially at the great centres, they took at the beginning large quantities of land which, at the time, were supposed to be far beyond any future possible want.

Experience, however, has demonstrated that this property is absolutely necessary for the safe and economical management of the Company's business.

These properties were acquired on very reasonable terms, either by private bargain or by legal process. During the twenty-five years since most of them were taken, there has been a vast increase of value caused generally by the rise in real estate, and particularly by the developments due to your road.

We have considered this subject in minute detail, and with special care and caution. We have also employed experts in real estate at the important points, whose reports, with those of the officers of the Company, and our own examinations and inquiries, are the joint guides for the judgment we have formed.

To state each property separately, its location and extent, for what purpose used, when, how, from whom, and on what terms obtained, is impossible within the limits of this report, for it would require a volume, nor is it either necessary or desirable. The voluminous papers containing all this information we shall place in the archives of the Company, where they will be useful for reference. We accomplish all the objects of your resolution on this subject by presenting the following summary.

It is proper to add that this statement does not include the lands used for the bed of the road, and that the whole of the property in West Philadelphia, including building-lots on Market and other streets, is valued at the low sum of about $10,000 per acre.

Real Estate owned by the Pennsylvania Railroad Company.

Philadelphia Division (Philadelphia to Harrisburg).

Number of properties, 253.
Number of acres of land, $1022\frac{70}{100}$.
Estimated present value of land, . . . $8,965,754 75

Middle Division (Harrisburg to Altoona).

Number of properties, 183.
Number of acres of land, $4658\tfrac{75}{100}$.
Estimated present value of land, . . . $1,785,808 00

Pittsburg Division (Altoona to Pittsburg).

Number of properties, 328.
Number of acres of land, $2827\tfrac{30}{100}$.
Estimated present value of land, . . . 7,790,554 08

Hollidaysburg and Morrison's Cove Branches.

Number of properties, 12.
Number of acres of land, $\tfrac{51}{100}$.
Estimated present value of land, . . . 5,080 00

Indiana Branch.

Number of properties, 9.
Number of acres of land, $133\tfrac{97}{100}$.
Estimated present value of land, . . . 8,826 00

Summary of Real Estate.

Total number of properties, 785.
Total number of acres, $8733\tfrac{23}{100}$.
Estimated value of lands, ... 18,556,022 83

2. Machinery and Tools.

Philadelphia Division, ...	$188,370 00
Middle Division, ...	938,400 00
Pittsburg Division, ...	143,650 00
Total, ...	$1,270,420 00

We have made no addition or deduction in this article, and merely include it as an item of property. The above statement shows the cash value, irrespective of cost, which, indeed, it would be impossible to determine, in consequence of perpetual changes, renewals, wear and tear, and repairs.

3. *Equipment.*

The locomotives and cars have been carefully examined and valued as of December 31st, 1873, when the report of the Directors was made up, with the following result:—

4,201 box cars, eight-wheeled, at	$575,	$2,415,575	
2,000 stock cars, eight-wheeled, at	550,	1,100,000	
7,877 gondola cars, eight-wheeled, at	500,	3,938,500	
1,508 coal cars, eight-wheeled, at	475,	716,300	
213 dump cars, eight-wheeled, at	375,	79,875	
62 cabin cars, eight-wheeled, at	475,	29,450	
25 derrick cars, eight-wheeled, at	475,	11,875	
13 tool and paint cars, eight-wheeled, at	500,	6,500	
1 snow-plow, eight-wheeled, at	500,	500	
15,900 Total,			$8,298,575
543 coal cars, four-wheeled, at	$275,	$149,325	
356 cabin cars, four-wheeled, at	300,	106,800	
128 dump cars, four-wheeled, at	225,	28,800	
365 hand cars, four-wheeled, at	60,	21,900	
400 push cars, four-wheeled, at	30,	12,000	
6 derrick cars, four-wheeled, at	200,	1,200	
1,798 Total,			320,025
319 passenger cars, first class, at	$4,500,	$1,435,500	
66 passenger cars, second class, at	2,750,	181,500	
136 mail, baggage, and express cars, at	1,750,	238,000	
521 Total,			1,855,000
151 passenger locomotives, at	$10,500,	$1,585,500	
595 freight locomotives, at	11,500,	6,842,500	
133 distributing and shifting locomotives, at	9,000,	1,197,000	
879 Total,			9,625,000
Grand total,			$20,098,600

4. Road-bed, Track, Bridges, and Telegraph Lines.

We have found it difficult to make a reliable estimate of the present value of the road-bed and track, bridges, and telegraph lines, and have therefore preferred to take the balance standing on the books of the Company for the construction of the railroad between Harrisburg and Pittsburg, including branches to Indiana and Hollidaysburg (in all two hundred and seventy-six miles), also for the cost of stations, warehouses, shops, and shop-machinery, on the whole road from Philadelphia to Pittsburg, viz., $19,610,223.81, and add to it such amounts as have been, from 1855 to 1873, inclusive, charged to expense account, which might have been properly charged to construction. It is well known that this has been the well-advised and systematic custom of your officers, thereby keeping down the capital account.

Taking the sums so charged during the past nineteen years from the books of the Company, we find they amount to $36,133,637.19, and consist generally of excess of earnings over dividends and interest, which was required by the charter to be credited to construction account on the completion of a single track to Pittsburg, in 1855; amounts paid the State from time to time on account of the purchase of the Philadelphia and Columbia Railroad; amounts expended for rebuilding and straightening the Philadelphia and Columbia Railroad, the Harrisburg and Lancaster Railroad, and parts of the main line west of the mountains; for building the Delaware Extension, with its wharves and elevator; for the substitution of steel for iron rails and of greater weight per yard; iron for wooden bridges, and a very large increase in length of road-bed, track, sidings, and yard accommodations.

The present increased value of the road-bed, track, buildings, &c. will be the more readily shown by bringing together the items upon which we have placed a value, and comparing such value with the cost at the time they were made, laid, and built, in the following manner:—

Road-bed, track, bridges, stations, warehouses, buildings, shops, shop-machinery, and telegraph lines, including the Philadelphia and Columbia Railroad,	$55,743,861 00
Equipment of road,	20,098,600 00
Real estate,	18,556,022 83
Total present estimated value,	$94,398,483 83
The amount charged in the General Account is	48,571,808 18
Showing an increase of valuation of	$45,826,675 65
This large increase is due to an increased expenditure on the road and branches between Philadelphia and Pittsburg, over and above what is shown in the general account, of	$28,964,876 62
In the value of equipment of	4,764,885 56
In the value of real estate of	12,096,913 47
Amounting in all to	$45,826,675 65

And exceeds the estimate in the last annual report $12,471,052.03, chiefly due to our increased estimate of the value of real estate and the amounts expended on the Philadelphia and Columbia and the Harrisburg and Lancaster Railroads.

Taking the real cost of road, embracing nine hundred and ninety-four miles single track, as above, at $55,743,861, it gives an average cost of $45,436 for one mile of single track, which is below the average of the best roads, but which is represented on your books at an average cost of $19,730 per mile, making a total cost of $19,610,223.81.

This vast increase of real values is not to be accounted an absolute present gain, because all the road-bed and most of the land is necessary for the operations of the Company, and cannot, therefore, be sold. It is property available and essential for use, but not convertible in mass. It yields revenue because it is part of the principal from which the income of the road is derived; besides, these increased values may be considered with reference to—

First.—The advantages which they give over rival roads because of the lesser comparative capital invested to obtain the same objects.

Second. Railroad incomes rise in proportion to decrease of capital; it follows that as most of the cost of the material structure of your railroad, with all its land, buildings, and appurtenances, was at very low prices, you have now all the advantage of the difference, for your present charges for the transportation of persons and property are based on the present purchasing power of money, whereas your investments were made when that power was much greater.

Third.—The large extent of land owned by the Company at important points, and especially at Philadelphia and Pittsburg, gives you a commanding position in reference to other roads, and will be the source of considerable revenue in the shape of rent. Experience has shown the advantages resulting from concentrating diverging railway lines in central depots, and of course the lines which use these depots pay the company who owns them. We do not attempt to estimate this revenue, but as rent is mainly based on invested capital, the Company will have all the advantage of the increased value of property thus used.

Fourth.—Another advantage and source of profit is the leasing of that portion of the property of the Company not required for immediate use, which, being rented to other persons, yielded to your treasury in 1873 a sum of $82,497. This sum seems too small considering the extent of the rented property, and we especially commend to the Directors an examination as to the terms and persons who are the tenants and occupants of the property of the Company.

Fifth.—A most important element in estimating the advantages of the comparatively small cost of your road and land is the additional security which it gives to bondholders and stockholders. As this is absolute gain, it gives to the bondholder the same percentage of increased security, and to the stockholder the like increase of capital.

Sixth.—It will be observed that we have not made any estimate of the increased value of buildings. It is certain that they are worth more than they cost; but there are several incomputable elements which would enter into arithmetical calculation, and which make it impossible to give even an approximate reliable estimate, and we therefore prefer to allow them to stand at their actual cost.

Stockholders have a right to know what their agents have done with their money, and inasmuch as we do not hesitate to state all errors and losses in the administration of the Company, justice demands that we should also state the gains resulting from their wisdom.

Aware of the tendency in most men's minds to exaggerate expectations of future and indefinite results, especially in matters of self-interest, we have been especially guarded against this error, and it is probable that, suspicious of imagination and rigid in judgment, we may have fallen into the opposite extreme. At all events, we are fully persuaded in our own minds that if caution can assure confidence we may fairly claim it, and we believe that the developments of time will more than justify our expectations, and will prove that we have been too cautious rather than too confident.

ARTICLE III.

THE LIABILITIES OF THE PENNSYLVANIA RAILROAD COMPANY AS ENDORSER, GUARANTOR, LESSEE, OR OTHERWISE, WITH THE RESULT OF THESE LIABILITIES IN 1873, AND AN ESTIMATE OF PROBABLE FUTURE CLAIMS ON ACCOUNT OF ENDORSEMENTS, &c.

Contingent Liabilities from which no Profit can be derived.

We herewith append a list of the liabilities of the Company as endorser or guarantor on the bonds of other corporations. It will be seen that in most cases the Company is guarantor of both principal and interest, and in one case of interest only, and it will also be observed that in no case is it guarantor for any other liability than mortgage bonds and rentals, and in most cases first liens upon the property mortgaged. In many cases the Company stands with others as co-guarantor, but we have charged the Company with the entire liability, although the co-guarantors are in many cases entirely responsible. For $6,500,000 the Northern Central has an equal liability with the Pennsylvania Railroad Company, and in the case of the $800,000 bonded debt of the Junction Railroad, the liability is divided with the Philadelphia, Wilmington and Baltimore and the Philadelphia and Reading. These guarantees amount to $33,983,000, and in the case of the Pennsylvania Canal, the Company guarantees $180,000 interest per annum on $3,000,000 of first mortgage bonds. This debt is but a small portion of the value of the canal, and its profits are abundant to pay the interest and leave a large surplus.

Detailed Statement of Contingent Liabilities on Bonds.

Western Pennsylvania Railroad,	$1,158,600
Connecting Railroad,	991,000
Philadelphia and Erie Railroad,	10,000,000
Chartiers Railway,	475,000
Susquehanna Coal Company,	1,300,000
Allegheny Valley Low-Grade,	9,059,000
Allegheny Valley Low-Grade*,	3,500,000
American Steamship,	1,500,000
Pittsburg, Virginia and Charleston,	700,000
Baltimore and Potomac,†,	3,000,000
Baltimore and Potomac tunnel bonds,	1,500,000
Junction Railroad‡,	800,000
Total amount of bonds, principal and interest guaranteed,	$33,983,600

Pennsylvania Canal—interest ($180,000) guaranteed on $3,000,000, but not the principal.

Yearly Liabilities as Lessee and Guarantor.

Before commenting upon these liabilities, we here present the following statement of them:—

---

* Northern Central and Philadelphia and Erie co-guarantors with Pennsylvania Railroad Company on this three and a half millions of bonds.

† Northern Central co-guarantor with Pennsylvania Railroad Company.

‡ Philadelphia, Wilmington and Baltimore and Philadelphia and Reading co-guarantors with Pennsylvania Railroad Company.

(1.) STATEMENT OF ANNUAL LIABILITIES OF THE PENNSYLVANIA RAILROAD COMPANY AS GUARANTOR FOR AND ON ACCOUNT OF THE ROADS NAMED BELOW WEST OF PITTSBURG.

Pittsburg, Fort Wayne and Chicago Railway.

1873. Total annual rental, ... $2,617,177 24

Also the following, in connection with the lease of the above road:—

New Castle and Beaver Valley Railroad.

Leased for forty per cent. of gross earnings. Minimum rental, ... 140,435 79

Lawrence Railroad.

Leased for forty per cent. of gross earnings. Minimum rental, ... 75,752 96

Indianapolis and St. Louis Railroad.

Interest on debt—
Seven per cent. on $3,000,000,	$210,000
Eight per cent. on $500,000, .	40,000
St. Louis, Alton and Terre Haute, ...	150,000

400,000 00

NOTE.—The Pennsylvania Company is owner of one-half of the capital stock of the Indianapolis and St. Louis Railroad Company, which is the lessee of the St. Louis, Alton and Terre Haute Railroad; and, as the assignee of the lease of the Pittsburg, Fort Wayne and Chicago Railway, is liable for one-third of the minimum rental of the St. Louis, Alton and Terre Haute Railroad, the other two-thirds being guaranteed by the Indianapolis, Cincinnati and Lafayette Railroad Company, the Cleveland, Columbus, Cincinnati and Indianapolis Railway Company, and the Lake Shore and Michigan Southern Railway Companies, each for itself.

Carried forward, $3,233,365 99

Brought forward, $3,233,365 99

Grand Rapids and Indiana Railroad.

Interest on one-half of debt, seven per cent. on $4,000,000, (gold,) 280,000 00

Total liabilities in connection with the lease of the Pittsburg, Fort Wayne and Chicago Railroad, ... $3,513,365 99

Cleveland and Pittsburg Railroad.

Total annual rental, ... 1,226,834 47

Erie and Pittsburg Railroad.

Total annual rental, ... 380,626 00

Jeffersonville, Madison and Indianapolis Railroad.

Total annual rental, ... 532,651 70

Little Miami Railroad.

Total annual rental, ... 723,908 80

NOTE.—The interest on the street connection bonds is the whole of such interest, the bonds being executed jointly by the Little Miami and the Cincinnati and Indiana Railroad Companies. The Little Miami, or the Pittsburg, Cincinnati and St. Louis Railway Company as the lessee of Little Miami, is liable to the bondholders for the whole interest in the event of the failure to pay by the Indianapolis, Cincinnati and Lafayette Railroad Company. At present such interest is provided for in the proportion of sixty per cent. by the Pittsburg, Cincinnati and St. Louis Railway Company, and forty per cent. by the Indianapolis, Cincinnati and Lafayette Railroad Company.

Carried forward, $6,377,386 96

Brought forward, $6,377,386 96

Columbus, Chicago and Indiana Central Railway.

Leased for thirty per cent. of gross earnings, (but interest at seven per cent. guaranteed on $15,821,000 of debt secured by first mortgages,) as shown for 1873, . . 1,343,342 05

St. Louis, Vandalia and Terre Haute Railroad.

Leased by Terre Haute and Indianapolis Railroad Company for thirty per cent. of gross earnings, with a contingent liability for five per cent. more in case the expense of operating the road should fall to sixty-five per cent.; but the interest on the mortgage debt is guaranteed in the proportion of one-fifth by the Terre Haute and Indianapolis Railroad Company, two-fifths by the Columbus, Chicago and Indiana Central Railway Company, and two-fifths by the Pittsburg, Cincinnati and St. Louis Railway Company. The liability, therefore, of the Pittsburg, Cincinnati and St. Louis Railway Company, for herself and as lessee, is four-fifths of the interest on the mortgage debt. Seven per cent. on $4,500,000=$315,000, four-fifths of which is 252,000 00

Newport and Cincinnati Bridge.

Guarantee of one-half of $75,000. Minimum traffic, ... 37,500 00

Carried forward, $8,010,229 01

                              Brought forward, $8,010,229 01

Indianapolis and Vincennes Railroad.

Interest on mortgage debt, seven
   per cent. on $1,700,000, . . $119,000
Six per cent. on $1,450,000, · .   87,000
                                              ―――――   206,000 00

       Total, ... $8,216,229 01

(2.) STATEMENT OF ANNUAL LIABILITIES OF THE PENNSYLVANIA RAILROAD COMPANY UNDER LEASES OF ROADS EAST OF PITTSBURG AND ERIE, ALSO, ON ACCOUNT OF GUARANTEES ON BONDS OF LEASED AND CONTROLLED ROADS EAST OF PITTSBURG AND ERIE.

Western Pennsylvania Railroad.

Leased by the Pennsylvania Railroad Company to be operated at cost, handing balance of receipts over to the lessor. (Net receipts for 1873, $348,968.77.)

Pennsylvania Railroad Company guarantees principal and interest of $800,000 first mortgage main line bonds, six per cent., $48,000.

Pennsylvania Railroad Company guarantees principal and interest of $358,600 first mortgage Pittsburg Branch bonds, six per cent., $21,600.

Connecting Railroad.

Leased by the Philadelphia and Trenton Railroad Company at an annual rental of six per cent. on its bonds and stock= $142,965.90. This amount is included in rental of United Railroads of New Jersey next mentioned.

Pennsylvania Railroad Company guarantees principal and interest of $991,000 first mortgage bonds, six per cent., $59,460.

United Railroads and Canal of New Jersey.

Leased by the Pennsylvania Railroad Company at an annual rental, which amounted in 1873 to $3,117,020.24. (Loss in 1873, $685,689.70.)

Bald Eagle Valley Railroad.

Leased by the Pennsylvania Railroad Company, who pay to lessor forty per cent. of the gross receipts after deducting all tonnage taxes. (Net profits in 1873, $8228.57.)

Bedford and Bridgeport Railroad.

Leased by the Pennsylvania Railroad Company to be operated at cost, handing balance of receipts over to lessor. (Loss in 1873, $3252.72.)

Danville, Hazleton and Wilkesbarre Railroad.

Leased by the Pennsylvania Railroad Company to be operated at cost, balance of receipts to be applied to payment of coupons on $1,400,000 bonds. If not sufficient, the Pennsylvania Railroad Company purchases coupons and holds them as against the mortgage.

Pennsylvania Railroad Company guarantees to purchase coupons. (Seven per cent. on $1,400,000=$98,000.)

East Brandywine and Waynesburg Railroad.

Leased by the Pennsylvania Railroad Company, paying to lessor not less than thirty-three and one-third per cent. of the gross earnings to meet interest on bonds. (Loss in 1873, $7466.54.)

Ebensburg and Cresson Railroad.

Leased by the Pennsylvania Railroad Company to be operated at cost, balance of receipts being devoted to paying interest on $80,000 mortgage bonds, if sufficient; if not, then *pro rata*. (Loss in 1873, $1910.58.)

Harrisburg, Portsmouth, Mt. Joy and Lancaster Railroad.

Leased by the Pennsylvania Railroad Company, rental being (six per cent. on bonds, seven per cent. on stock, taxes, and organization) in 1873, $132,651.46.

Lewisburg, Centre and Spruce Creek Railroad.

Leased by the Pennsylvania Railroad Company to be operated at cost, balance of gross earnings being devoted to paying interest on bonded debt. (Net profits in 1873, $6983.94 on eleven miles of road.)

Mifflin and Centre County Railroad.

Leased by the Pennsylvania Railroad Company to be operated at cost, balance of gross receipts being applied to rent ($330) of Tuscarora bridge, and to payment of interest on $100,000 mortgage bonds, if sufficient; if not, then *pro rata*. (Loss in 1873, $13,382.59.)

Newry Railroad.

Leased by the Pennsylvania Railroad Company to be operated at cost, applying balance to paying cost of completion of road and appurtenances. (Loss in 1873, $2904.02.)

Sunbury and Lewistown Railroad.

Leased by the Pennsylvania Railroad Company to be operated at cost, paying over surplus to lessor.

Tyrone and Clearfield Railroad.

Leased by the Pennsylvania Railroad Company to be operated at cost, paying over surplus to lessor. (Net profits in 1873, $62,244.35.)

South West Pennsylvania Railroad.

Leased by the Pennsylvania Railroad Company to be operated at cost, paying over balance to lessor. (Net profits in 1873, $56,746.98.)

Pennsylvania and Delaware Railroad.

Leased by the Pennsylvania Railroad Company to be operated at cost, paying over balance to lessor. (Loss in 1873, $30,912.52.)

Philadelphia and Erie Railroad.

Leased by the Pennsylvania Railroad Company to be operated at cost to work it, balance being devoted to organization, interest on bonds, sinking fund under one of the mortgages, then surplus to lessor, after deducting moneys loaned and advances made by lessee.

Pennsylvania Railroad Company guarantees principal and interest of $2,000,000 dollar bonds, six per cent.,	$120,000
Pennsylvania Railroad Company guarantees principal and interest account $3,000,000 sterling bonds, six per cent.,	180,000
Pennsylvania Railroad Company guarantees principal and interest of $5,000,000 gold bonds, six per cent.,	300,000
Total,	$600,000

Chartiers Railway.

Leased by Pittsburg, Cincinnati and St. Louis Railway Company for what it costs, paying balance to lessor. (Net receipts, 1873, $18,205.78.)

Pennsylvania Railroad Company guarantees principal and interest of $475,000 first mortgage bonds, seven per cent., ... $33,250

Pennsylvania Canal.

Pennsylvania Railroad Company guarantees the interest on first and general mortgage bonds, amounting to $3,000,000, at six per cent., . 180,000

Allegheny Valley Railroad.

Pennsylvania Railroad Company guarantees principal and interest of $9,059,000 first mortgage "low-grade" bonds, seven per cent., . . 634,130
$3,500,000 second mortgage "low-grade" bonds, five per cent., ... 175,000
—the Northern Central and Philadelphia and Erie Companies joining in the last named.

Susquehanna Coal Company.

Pennsylvania Railroad Company guarantees principal and interest of $1,300,000 bonds, at six per cent., ... $78,000

American Steamship Company.

Pennsylvania Railroad Company guarantees principal and interest of $1,500,000 bonds, at six per cent., ... 90,000

Pittsburg, Virginia and Charleston Railroad.

Pennsylvania Railroad Company guarantees principal and interest of $700,000 first mortgage bonds, at seven per cent., gold, . . . $49,000

Baltimore and Potomac Railroad.

Pennsylvania Railroad Company guarantees principal and interest of $1,500,000 "Tunnel bonds," at six per cent., gold, ... 90,000
$3,000,000 "Main Line bonds," at six per cent., gold, ... 180,000
The latter in connection with the Northern Central Railway Company.

Junction Railroad.

The Pennsylvania Railroad Company, the Philadelphia, Wilmington and Baltimore Railroad Company, and the Philadelphia and Reading Railroad Company, guarantee the principal and interest on $500,000 first mortgage bonds, six per cent., ... $30,000
$300,000 second mortgage bonds, six per cent., . 18,000

Total, ... $48,000

An examination of the above-mentioned leases and guarantees shows that, in addition to the guarantees of bonds heretofore alluded to, there are leases of two entirely different kinds.

The *first* are a class of leases wherein the Pennsylvania Railroad Company stipulates to operate the road at cost and pay over to the lessors all surplus profits, and not obligating itself in any way to pay more, nor in fact assuming any obligation other than to deal honestly. This class of leases we shall not stop to consider, as they form no part of the liabilities or assets of the Company.

The *second* and important class are those wherein the Pennsylvania Railroad Company stipulates to pay an annual fixed rental. These are as follows:—

Name of Road.	Yearly Guaranteed Rent.
United Railroads and Canal of New Jersey,	$3,117,020 24
Harrisburg, Portsmouth, Mt. Joy and Lancaster,	132,651 46
Pittsburg, Fort Wayne and Chicago,	2,617,177 24
New Castle and Beaver Valley,	140,435 79
Lawrence Railroad,	75,752 96
Erie and Pittsburg,	380,626 00
Cleveland and Pittsburg,	1,337,353 51
Jeffersonville, Madison and Indianapolis,	535,235 60
Indianapolis and Vincennes,	206,000 00
Indianapolis and St. Louis,	707,065 46
Columbus, Chicago and Indiana Central,	1,343,342 05
Little Miami,	710,769 94
St. Louis, Vandalia and Terre Haute,	271,395 16
Chartiers Railway,	35,000 00
Total rentals guaranteed,	$11,609,819 41

The operations of these roads for the year 1873 and the profit and loss account show the following results:—

Name of Road.	Earnings.	Expenses.
United Railroads of New Jersey,	$11,255,062 81	$8,823,732 27
Harrisburg, Portsmouth, Mt. Joy and Lancaster,	. . . .	. . . .
Pittsburg, Fort Wayne and Chicago,	9,619,074 36	6,097,041 99
New Castle and Beaver Valley,	351,089 48	158,574 75
Lawrence Railroad,	189,382 38	113,371 05
Erie and Pittsburg,	1,165,292 62	680,893 88
Cleveland and Pittsburg,	3,671,735 25	1,874,722 15
Jeffersonville, Madison and Indianapolis,	1,437,576 91	991,377 03
Indianapolis and Vincennes,	253,784 14	191,647 13
Indianapolis and St. Louis,	2,097,528 46	1,406,619 33
Little Miami,	1,401,547 82	1,239,530 05
Columbus, Chicago and Indiana Central,	4,477,806 84	4,244,624 12
Chartiers Railway,	61,558 62	43,267 44
	$35,981,439 69	
Harrisburg, Portsmouth, Mt. Joy and Lancaster, guaranteed rent,	132,651 46	
Gross earnings and expenses,	$36,113,091 15	$25,865,401 19
Add annual rentals, as above,*	. . . .	11,609,819 41
Total expenses,	. . . .	$37,475,220 60
Deduct gross earnings,	. . . .	36,113,091 15
Total net loss,	. . . .	$1,362,129 45

* In addition to the above, the Pennsylvania Railroad Company is bound by an agreement with the Northern Central Railway Company to pay one-half the loss, if any, in operating the Williamsport and Elmira Railroad. The half for 1873 was $108,000.

It is proper to add that the above loss on bonds and leases, excepting that of the United Railroads of New Jersey, have been met by the Pennsylvania Company and the Pittsburg, Cincinnati and St. Louis Railway Company from their own resources.

In estimating the value of these leases, it must be borne in mind that railroads have two classes of owners, viz., bondholders, who accept a fixed yearly interest, and stockholders, who receive all present and future profits beyond the amount due to bondholders. In making these leases, each party to them is supposed to have been benefited. The stockholders of the leased roads no doubt expected to receive *more* money as rent than they were at the time of leasing receiving as dividends, thereby enabling them to realize at once the price which their stock would have been worth at some future time had they retained possession of their road.

The Pennsylvania Railroad Company, in making these leases, expected to derive revenue from two sources—first and immediate was the business that would be received on the main line from the leased roads; second and prospective were the profits expected to be derived from future and increased traffic. Hence it is not strange that as the most of these leases have been made within a period of five years, the results of their operation should be a loss; while the steady diminution of this loss shows that, in negotiating these leases, the officers of the Company were correct in supposing that there would be a future when a direct gain would result from them. For it needs no argument to demonstrate that increase of population produces increased consumption, accompanied with increased railroad traffic.

The increase in the traffic of the leased roads west of Pittsburg has been, within five years, over $6,000,000, and this too under diminished rates, while the direct losses on all these roads—including the United Railroads of New Jersey—for 1873 was $1,362,129.45; but we believe the year 1874 will demonstrate that the time has come when the Pennsylvania Railroad Company will receive yearly increased profits from some of its leased lines.

The operations of these roads for the six months ending June 30th, 1874, as compared with the corresponding period in 1873, show the following results:—

Western roads, net earnings, 1874,	$3,978,708 09
Western roads, " " 1873,	3,928,363 70
Increase in net earnings,	$50,344 39
United Railroads of N. J., net earnings, 1874,	$927,915 31
United Railroads of N. J., " " 1873,	327,078 04
Increase in net earnings,	$600,837 27

Increase in net earnings on western roads,	$50,344 39	
Increase on United Railroads of New Jersey,	600,837 27	
		$651,181 66
Deduct Pittsburg, Cincinnati and St. Louis Railway, as the profits of that company go into its own treasury,		168,166 28
Total increased net earnings on the Western and New Jersey Railroads, for the first six months of 1874,		$483,015 38

For details of which, see Appendixes B and C.

The Pennsylvania Company shows increased net earnings from other sources than leases for the first six months of 1874, over the net earnings for the same period in 1873, of $1,006,185.74.

Should the operations for the last six months of 1874 produce no better results than the last six months of 1873, still the leased lines will show a much less loss than in 1873, and may show a surplus. The above, we think, demonstrates that while the New Jersey lines will hereafter pay a profit, the western lines will be no burden, and you will have in addition whatever gain may result from their furnishing profitable traffic and travel to your main line.

Combining the figures we have given above of your liabilities as guarantor on bonds and leases besides your own, it would be—

For lines east of Pittsburg, an annual rental of $5,646,090 93
For lines west of Pittsburg, . . . 8,216,229 01

Total amount for year, ... $13,862,319 94

On which we estimate for 1874 an absolute loss as guarantor of but $280,000, whilst moneys may have to be advanced to the extent of $1,000,000 on account of your guarantees to other roads, the same becoming a charge against these companies.

We confess to an agreeable surprise in coming to this conclusion. It should allay any fears on the part of the stockholders of the Pennsylvania Railroad Company that the liberal use of its credit had imposed on it damaging liabilities, and we congratulate you on the happy escape from the injuries in which the spirit of expansion and undue extension of railroads seemed likely to involve the main lines of railroad, a continuance of which for a few years longer would certainly have made bankrupt every trunk line in the country that indulged in this policy.

ARTICLE IV.

An Inquiry into the Policy, Groups, and Results of all the Railways and Canals owned or controlled by the Pennsylvania Railroad Company.

To facilitate and systematize this inquiry, we divide the railways into the Western and Eastern Groups. The Western Group, embracing the railways west of Pittsburg, we again divide into the Fort Wayne or Northern system, and the Pittsburg, Cincinnati and St. Louis or Southern system. The Eastern Group embraces the railways east of Pittsburg and Erie, and is called the Eastern or Pennsylvania system, in contradistinction to the Western system, and for convenience we include in this system the interests held south of Baltimore and Cairo.

The early policy of your Company was, and still is, to encourage the building of branches along its main line, and to make such business connections with other roads within the Commonwealth as would attract the trade of the State over your line to the city of Philadelphia. In carrying out this policy, such lines as the Western Pennsylvania, Bald Eagle Valley, Clearfield, Southern Pennsylvania, and Blair County Railways were aided, and interests taken in them to develop the local trade of your road.

It was also found to be necessary to acquire interests, first, in the Northern Central Railway, to keep the port of Baltimore open to trade and travel between that city and the West over your line; and, second, the Cumberland Valley Railroad, to turn the products of that rich valley to Philadelphia over your road; and, third, the Philadelphia and Erie Railroad. By leasing it much of the trade of the country dependent on that line is secured to the city of Philadelphia.

For some years you kept aloof from investments in western railroads, trusting to business alliances, mutual benefits, and advantages offered to western roads, and the absolute strength of your main line to secure a fair proportion of the western trade and travel. True to this wise policy, no interest had been taken in the West except in the Pittsburg, Fort Wayne and Chicago Railway, which was mainly done to secure its completion to Chicago, and which being accomplished at a favorable moment of high prices for the stock, your interest in that road was sold out at a large profit.

But subsequently the Pittsburg, Fort Wayne and Chicago Railway Company considered their road long enough, as a base line, to have an independent eastern connection, and your Company were forced to prepare another outlet to the West, which resulted in commencing the exceedingly expensive piece of railway from Pittsburg to Steubenville, to make a connection via the Steubenville and Newark line and the Little Miami Railroad to Cincinnati, and by other lines to St. Louis. A little later new interests, decidedly averse to yours, seemed likely to get control of the Pittsburg, Fort Wayne and Chicago line, and your Directors felt themselves obliged to acquire control of the Columbus, Chicago and Indiana Central line to Chicago; after the acquisition of which by you, the stockholders of the Pittsburg, Fort Wayne and Chicago line quickly recognized their true interest in leasing their lines to your Company, which was a responsible one, rather than to another of more questionable ability.

It is easy, now, to see the error of disposing of your interest in the Pittsburg, Fort Wayne and Chicago Railway, instead of taking control of it, when it could have been obtained at a less cost. This line held the strategic position. With it the Pennsylvania Railroad Company could have largely influenced and controlled the trade and travel of the country south of it, your only competitor being the Baltimore and Ohio Railroad.

Your Company being so far committed in the West, it was but natural—affected as the whole country was with the fever of railroad building, and constantly provoked by the efforts of the other trunk lines to interfere with the country which your Company thought belonged to them geographically—that they should partake of the same spirit, and, with grand ideas, form a plan or policy to reach all important points in the West with their lines; and this they have done; then followed the lease of the Little Miami Railroad and its branches, the Muskingum Valley Railroad, the building of the Vandalia road to St. Louis, the Indianapolis and Vincennes road, the three grand bridges over the Ohio river at Steubenville, Cincinnati, and Louisville, the control of the Jeffersonville, Madison and Indianapolis, the Cleveland, Mount Vernon and Delaware road, and many other branches, which give your Company a giant hold on the West. Commencing on Lake Erie, you reach with your lines the ports of Erie, Cleveland, Ashtabula, Toledo; and going North, the timber of Michigan; the cities of Cincinnati, Chicago, and St. Louis each with two lines; Cairo (by aid of Vincennes and Cairo Railroad), New Albany, Jeffersonville, Madison, and Louisville, on the Ohio; while these lines encircle the country directly tributary to them, they also have their feelers pointing to a greater circle outside, and drawing trade and travel to the main lines.

You will agree with us that the conception was grand, attractive, and likely, in times of great speculation, to captivate the most prudent. This grand conception appealed both to sentiment and interest with almost irresistible power, and it is not marvelous that every effort was made to put it into practical effect.

Having thus briefly sketched the circumstances that gave rise to the policy of your Company in the West, we will now consider the methods of management of your interests in the railways west of Pittsburg.

1. Western Group.

These roads are managed through the organization known as *The Pennsylvania Company*, the control of the management of which is secured by a majority of the stock being held by you, or by that company in your interest, and also by leasing from other companies lines which you control.

The Pennsylvania Company was originated and organized by your Company as a medium through which to make the best working organization for the Northern Group of lines west of Pittsburg. By centralizing the management, it was thought those roads could be more effectively managed, and their interests more readily harmonized. Whether this was the best policy we shall not now consider, for the Pennsylvania Company is so intimately connected with those lines as manager of some and lessee of others, and as owner of real estate and rolling stock, &c., that its existence had better be continued. It would have been well if it could have been arranged for that company to have sufficient capital to manage its own finances, independently of the aid of the Pennsylvania Railroad Company.

The capital of the Pennsylvania Company is $11,360,900, of which $8,000,000 is held as a preferred stock by the Pennsylvania Railroad Company, in exchange for securities and leases conveyed to it by the Pennsylvania Railroad Company.

This stock is entitled to a dividend of six per cent. per annum, and to a proportionate increase as profits may be divided over that rate. Its practical organization dates from April 1st, 1872.

The Pennsylvania Company, in 1873, purchased the property of the Union (Star) Line for $3,000,000, payable in their own stock. In addition to this stock there is the amount of $360,900 held by different persons.

This introduction of new stockholders suggests an important question. If the object of your Company in organizing the Pennsylvania Company was simply to have a better means of managing some of your western interests, and these interests are to be managed solely or primarily in the interest of your Company, is it judicious to introduce other stockholders whose interest may at times clash or interfere with yours?

It is not difficult to see that these interferences of interest may frequently occur, and so largely as to create great trouble. In fact, the Pennsylvania Company cannot be well managed for the purposes for which it was organized without ignoring the interests of its other stockholders.

Again, having other stockholders in the company affects the free working of the Pennsylvania Company. The policy of your Company may change, and it may be desirable to close the Pennsylvania Company, and we therefore suggest that your Board of Directors be recommended to re-examine the subject and see if an arrangement cannot be made by which your Company shall become the sole owners of the stock of the Pennsylvania Company.

Fort Wayne or Northern System.

The lines managed by the Pennsylvania Company are as follows:—

	Miles.	Miles.
1. The Pittsburg, Fort Wayne and Chicago Railway, extending from Pittsburg to Chicago,		468.3
And under this company, the New Castle and Beaver Valley Railroad,		14.9
The Lawrence Railroad,		20.4

NOTE.—The Pittsburg, Fort Wayne and Chicago Railway was leased by the Pennsylvania Railroad Company and the lease transferred to the Pennsylvania Company.

2. The Erie and Pittsburg Railroad, extending from a point on New Castle and Beaver Valley Railroad to Girard, on the Lake Shore Railroad, ... 84
Branch at Erie, ... 2
— 86.

NOTE.—This line leased by Pennsylvania Railroad Company and transferred to the Pennsylvania Company.

3. The Cleveland and Pittsburg Railroad. This line extends from Rochester, in Pennsylvania, by way of Millville, Ohio, to Bridgeport and Cleveland, with other branches, . . . 202.

NOTE.—This line leased by Pennsylvania Railroad Company and transferred to Pennsylvania Company.

4. Ashtabula, Youngstown and Pittsburg Railroad, from Youngstown to Ashtabula, . . . 62.5

NOTE.—This line is worked at cost by Pennsylvania Company, but there is no responsibility or guaranty of dividend.

5. Mansfield, Coldwater and Lake Michigan Railroad is to extend from Mansfield Junction, on the Pittsburg, Fort Wayne and Chicago Railway, to Allegan, Michigan, two hundred and sixteen miles. The track is laid from Junction, seven miles west of Mansfield, to a point twenty-seven and three-quarter miles west of Tiffin, ... 65¾

Carried forward, 65¾ 854.1

	Miles.	Miles.
Brought forward,	65¾	854.1

Track is laid from Allegan to Grand Rapids and
    Indiana Railroad, ... $19\frac{7}{10}$

Total track laid on Mansfield, Coldwater and
    Lake Michigan Railroad, ...   85.5

NOTE.—This line is worked by Pennsylvania Company at cost.

6. Tiffin, Toledo and Eastern Railroad, . . 24
Woodville and Toledo Railroad, leased by Tiffin,
    Toledo and Eastern Railroad, . . . 18
                                              —— 42

NOTE.—Operated by Pennsylvania Company, for account of
Tiffin, Toledo and Eastern Railroad Company, at cost.

                                                    981.6

These roads, embracing 981.6 miles, are more properly the system of the Pennsylvania Company's lines; but with the lease of the Pittsburg, Fort Wayne and Chicago Railway there was also conveyed a contract with the Indianapolis and St. Louis Railroad, by which the Pennsylvania Railroad Company acquired one-half interest in this line, being the northern line between those cities, and therefore the accounts of this line come into the workings of the Pennsylvania Company. The result in 1873 was a loss of $8078.16, being one-half the total loss, the balance being paid by the Cleveland, Columbus, Cincinnati and Indianapolis Railway Company.

	Miles.	Miles.

7. The Indianapolis and St. Louis Railroad, In-
    dianapolis to Terre Haute, ... 72
Terre Haute to St. Louis, ... 189
Branch to Alton, ... 4
                                              —— 265

NOTE.—This interest was transferred to the Pennsylvania Company with the lease of the Pittsburg, Fort Wayne and Chicago Railway.

                            Carried forward,   265

	Miles.	Miles
Brought forward,		265

8. The Pennsylvania Company leases the Jeffersonville, Madison and Indianapolis Railroad, with the guarantees of the Pennsylvania Railroad Company. This line extends from Indianapolis to Louisville, ... 110

Madison to Columbus, ... 45

Columbus to Cambridge, ... 65
———— 220

9. The Indianapolis and Vincennes Railroad, extending between those points, . . . 117

NOTE.—Controlled by Pennsylvania Company, by majority of stock, and by paying interest on funded debt.

582

Making, with the northern system of . . . 981.6

Miles of railway operated by the Pennsylvania Company, ... 1,563.6

The amount of stock and bonds issued on these roads, and their floating and other indebtedness,* are—

Stock to amount of $44,020,140 35
Bonds to amount of 41,005,000 00
Floating and other indebtedness, . . . 2,572,196 22

Amounting in all to $87,597,336 57

With a cost per mile of road of $51,316.54.

We now add a table of the workings of these lines for 1873, showing the earnings, expenses, rental, profit, and loss.

---

* With the Cleveland, Mt. Vernon and Delaware Railroad, which has stock, $1,562,791.92; bonds, $2,300,000; debt, $362,643.08; total, $4,225,435. Length of road, 144 miles.

Summary of Results of Pennsylvania Company's Lines in 1873.

ROADS.	Gross Earnings.	Operating Expenses.	Net Earnings.	Rental.	Profit.	Loss.
Pittsburg, Fort Wayne and Chicago Railway,	$9,619,074 36	$6,097,041 99	$3,522,032 37	$2,617,177 24	$904,855 13	. . . .
New Castle and Beaver Valley Railroad . .	351,089 48	158,574 75	192,514 73	140,435 79	52,078 94	. . . .
Lawrence Railroad, ...	189,382 38	113,371 05	76,011 33	75,752 96	258 37	. . . .
Erie and Pittsburg Railroad, ...	1,165,292 62	680,893 88	484,398 74	380,626 00	103,772 74	. . . .
Mansfield, Coldwater and Lake Michigan Railroad, ...	57,264 12	54,994 49	2,269 63	. . . . . .	2,269 63	. . . .
Toledo, Tiffin and Eastern Railroad, . . .	48,279 80	40,998 58	7,281 22	. . . . . .	7,281 22	. . . .
Ashtabula, Youngstown and Pittsburg Railroad, ...	77,918 79	81,511 59	. . . . . .	. . . . . .	. . . . . .	$3,592 80
Cleveland and Pittsburg Railroad, ...	3,759,626 96	1,989,714 47	1,760,912 49	1,226,834 47	534,078 02	. . . .
Jeffersonville, Madison and Indianapolis Railroad	1,434,993 01	991,377 03	443,615 98	532,651 70	. . . . . .	89,035 72
Indianapolis and Vincennes Railroad, . . .	253,784 14	191,647 13	62,137 01	206,000 00	. . . . . .	143,862 99
	$16,947,705 66	$10,400,124 96	$6,551,173 50	$5,179,478 16	$1,604,594 05	$236,491 51

Net profit on the system, ... $1,368,102 54
Less one-half of loss on the Indianapolis and St. Louis road,   8,078 16

Amount of profit, ... $1,360,024 38

In the Appendix D will be found a statement showing the receipts of these lines for 1868 and 1873, and a comparison of the number of passengers and amount of tonnage. The table shows a satisfactory increase in most of the lines, and fully sanctions the remarks we have made.

A comparison of this table with the list of guarantees will show, first, that the Pennsylvania Railroad Company has not been called upon to pay any money on account of her leases or guarantees on the above lines; second, that the Pennsylvania Company, in working these lines, made a clear profit of $1,131,611.03.

We now take up the line of railway west of Pittsburg, operated in your interest through the control given to the Pennsylvania Company by its holding a majority of the stock of the Pittsburg, Cincinnati and St. Louis Railway Company. This, you will notice, involves no liability on the Pennsylvania Company other than that of loss on its stock, in which it is on a par with the other stockholders.

Pittsburg, Cincinnati and St. Louis or Southern System.

The lines of railway under the control of the Pittsburg, Cincinnati and St. Louis Railway Company, are the following:—

	Miles.
1. Pittsburg, Cincinnati and St. Louis Railway, extending from Pittsburg to Columbus.	
Made up of the Pittsburg end, extending from the Union depot to the Washington turnpike gate, owned by the Pennsylvania Railroad Company, and leased to the Pennsylvania Company,	$1\tfrac{1}{10}$
Steubenville and Newark, (Pittsburg, Cincinnati and St. Louis proper,)	$158\tfrac{9}{10}$
Carried forward,	160

	Miles.	Miles.
Brought forward,	160	

Newark to Columbus, (held in joint ownership with the Baltimore and Ohio Railroad,) . 33
Cadiz Branch, built by the Springfield and North-western Railroad, ... 8
                                                            ── 201

2. Chartiers Valley Railroad, leased to Pittsburg, Cincinnati and St. Louis Railway Company, and worked at cost, ... 22.8

Cincinnati and Muskingum Valley, leased to Pittsburg, Cincinnati and St. Louis Railway Company, but worked at cost, . . . 148.4

3. Little Miami Railroad, which consists of the Cincinnati and Springfield Railroad, the Dayton and Xenia Railroad, the Dayton and Richmond Railroad, and the Columbus and Xenia Railroad, in all 196.7

NOTE.—Leased by the Pittsburg, Cincinnati and St. Louis Railway Company, and guaranteed by the Pennsylvania Railroad Company.

4. The Columbus, Chicago and Indiana Central Railway, extending from Columbus to Chicago, through Richmond, and from Richmond to Indianapolis, and from Bradford Junction to near Logansport, and from Logansport to State Line, Illinois, . . 581.1

NOTE.—Leased by Pittsburg, Cincinnati and St. Louis Railway Company, and guaranteed by Pennsylvania Railroad Company.

                                                                1,150

This is the total length of line operated by the Pittsburg, Cincinnati and St. Louis Railway Company.

In addition to these roads as part of your railway system, we give a statement of the two bridges built in your interest over the Ohio river—the one at Cincinnati and the other at Louisville:—

1. The Newport and Cincinnati Bridge.

This bridge crosses the Ohio river at Cincinnati, and furnishes a railway connection between the roads north and south of that river converging at Cincinnati, and also gives a common road connection between the cities which give it its name.

Its cost is represented by—

Capital stock,	$1,200,000 00
Bonded debt, seven per cent.,	1,200,000 00
Floating debt,	812,766 55
	$3,212,766 55

Of which the Pennsylvania Railroad Company holds—

Capital stock,	$720,000 00
Mortgage bonds,	1,200,000 00
	$1,920,000 00

The capital stock was received as a bonus with the purchase of the bonds, and thus secures to the Pennsylvania Railroad Company the control of the bridge.

The Little Miami Railroad Company and others south are under a guarantee of $75,000 per annum to the bridge company for the railway traffic alone. The incidental and road traffic belongs to the bridge company. The business is developing and promises better results, although we fail to see any very good reasons for this outlay of capital by the Pennsylvania Railroad Company.

Gross receipts in 1873,	$76,975 88
Expenses and taxes in 1873,	23,866 50
Net receipts in 1873,	$53,109 38

2. *The Jeffersonville and Louisville Bridge.*

This company has a capital stock of	$1,500,000 00
Bonded debt,	800,000 00
	$2,300,000 00

And owns the track (one mile long) connecting the bridge (five thousand two hundred and ninety-four feet long) with the Louisville and Nashville Railroad station at Louisville.

Under the contract made with the bridge company by the railway companies using the bridge, the tolls are fixed at an amount to pay the cost of repairs, maintenance, taxes, interest on bonds, and sinking fund sufficient to pay them at maturity, and twelve per cent. on the capital stock.

The stock and bonds issued by the above-named roads and their floating and other debt* amount to—

Stock,	$33,359,128 49
Bonds,	47,654,760 25
Floating and other debt,	4,845,831 78
Total for 1318 miles,	$85,859,720 52
Or per mile of road costing	$65,040 00

We also add a table of the workings of these lines, showing earnings, expenses, rental, profit and loss.

---

* This includes the St. Louis, Vandalia and Terre Haute Railroad, with stock, $2,377,779.52; bonds, $5,490,000; debt, $250,557.97; total, $8,127,-337.49. Length of road, 168 miles.

Earnings, Expenses, Rentals, Profit and Loss of Pittsburg, Cincinnati and St. Louis or Southern System.

ROADS.	Earnings.	Expenses.	Net Earnings.	Rental.	Interest on funded debt.	Profit.	Loss.
Pittsburg, Cincinnati and St. Louis Railway,	$3,852,483 87	$3,425,800 31	$426,683 56	. . . . .	$669,790 00	. . . . .	$243,106 44
Chartiers Railway,	61,558 62	43,267 47	18,291 15	. . . . .	. . . . .	‡$18,291 15	. . . . .
Little Miami Railroad,	1,401,547 82	*1,239,530 05	162,017 77	$710,769 74	. . . . .	. . . . .	769,371 78
Columbus, Chicago and Indiana Central Railway,	4,477,806 84	†4,244,624 12	276,200 80	1,343,342 05	. . . . .	. . . . .	1,463,675 17
Cincinnati and Muskingum Valley Railroad,	443,216 68	423,787 48	19,419 20	. . . . .	. . . . .	§19,419 20	. . . . .

Showing a loss on their lines of . . . $2,476,153 39

* In expenses there was additional cost of discount on bonds given in liquidation of floating debt, ... $186,572 73
† To this is to be added discount on bonds given in liquidation of floating debt, ... 353,505 84
‡ Being worked at cost, this amount was paid to Chartiers Railway Company.
§ This amount has been placed to credit of that company to meet its funded debt.

56

In the Appendix D will be found a statement of gross earnings, number of tons of freight moved, and number of passengers carried by the above lines in 1868 and 1873. This table shows a very satisfactory increase in the earnings and business of each road, and also shows that if the same rates per ton had been received in 1873 that were in 1868 the financial result would have been much more favorable and shown a profit to the Company.

The loss on these lines had to be provided for by the Pittsburg, Cincinnati and St. Louis Railway Company first, and in case of their failing, became a charge against the Pennsylvania Railroad Company to the extent of $2,054,111.79.

It is but just to add here that some of these lines were taken by the Company in wretched order as to track, power, and equipment, and that a large amount has been annually expended in bringing up to a better standard the track, motive power, and cars, and we especially note the fine condition of all the western lines in these respects, showing the judicious expenditure of money. In 1873, such was the anticipated increase of business expected by these, as by all other roads, that large outlays were made to provide for the increasing trade, and the General Manager of this line of road reports that the capacity of the line in February, 1874, was fifteen per cent. greater than in 1873, owing to the improvements and betterments placed on it during 1873. He estimates these improvements to have cost—

For road and superstructure, including new water stations, bridge, three hundred and forty-eight miles new track, and one hundred and sixty-eight miles new ballast,	$1,197,020 72
Motive power, including entire rebuilding of seventy-seven engines,	258,626 15
Carried forward,	$1,455,646 87

Brought forward,	$1,455,646 87
Cars, rebuilding passenger, baggage, and freight cars,	268,748 64
Amounting to	$1,724,395 51

6. The St. Louis, Vandalia and Terre Haute Railroad is almost wholly owned by the Pennsylvania Company, and is operated under a lease by the Terre Haute and Indianapolis Railway Company.

The net results to the Pennsylvania Company for the year 1873, after paying interest on bonds, &c., was a profit of $4805.64. Length of road, 168 miles.

The Cleveland, Mount Vernon and Delaware Railroad extends from Hudson, through Orrville, Millersburg, and Mount Vernon, to Columbus, with a branch to Massillon, a distance of one hundred and forty-four miles, with an intended branch from Millersburg to Dresden, on the Pittsburg, Cincinnati and St. Louis Railway, and connecting there with the Muskingum Valley Railroad.

The common stock issued amounts to	$1,390,100 00
Of this you hold, (received as the valuation of the road when re-organized,)	1,100,000 00
Leaving in other hands,	$290,100 00
The preferred stock issued amounts to	$451,450 00
Of this you hold and have paid for five thousand eight hundred and two shares, representing	290,100 00
Leaving in other hands,	$161,350 00
The bonds amount to	$2,300,000 00

From the main line we cannot expect more than its ability to pay its interest. If the branch is built to Dresden, which should have been done first, and a connection thus be made between the ores at Cleveland and the coal in the Hocking valley, a more profitable business will be done between Hudson and Millersburg.

Let us now bring these western roads together.

The profit on the Fort Wayne system was, for	1,563.6 miles,	$1,360,024 38
The profit on the St. Louis, Vandalia and Terre Haute line,	168.0 miles,	4,805 64
Total profit for	1,731.6 miles,	$1,364,830 02
The loss by the Southern system was, for	1,150.0 miles,	2,476,143 39
Total loss on lines for	2,881.6 miles,	$1,111,313 37
The Pennsylvania Company made a profit in 1873 from other sources of		1,076,296 27
Which would leave a net loss on all the lines west of Pittsburg of		$35,017 10

Or, by the admission of the estimate of the General Manager, as above given, into the statement, it would show as follows:—

Profits on the Fort Wayne system and the Vandalia Line,	$1,364,830 02
Profit of the Pennsylvania Company in 1873 from other sources,	1,076,296 27
Profit of Pennsylvania Company,	$2,441,126 29

But, as the Pennsylvania Railroad Company owns about eight-elevenths of the whole stock of the Pennsylvania Company, this stock would be represented by a profit of $1,775,360 00

Losses by the Southern system, ... $2,476,143 39

Less improvements made and charged to expenses, providing an increased capacity of fifteen per cent. on eleven hundred and fifty miles of railroad, ... 1,724,395 51
───────────
751,747 88
───────────
$1,023,612 12

Showing a net gain to the Pennsylvania Railroad Company of $1,023,612.12 as the final result of the operations for 1873,—very nearly enough to pay for the additions made to the track and equipment of the Southern system of roads.

We also bring together the length of the western roads and their capital, to show total investment:—

Northern System.

Length of roads, . . 1,563.6 miles, capital, $83,371,901 57

Southern System.

Length of roads, . . 1,150.0 miles, capital, 77,732,383 03

St. Louis, Vandalia and Terre Haute Railroad.

Length of road, . . 168.0 miles, 8,127,337 49
───────────
Carried forward, 2,881.6 miles, $169,231,622 09

               Brought forward, 2,881.6 miles, $169,231,622 09

Cleveland, Mt. Vernon and
  Delaware Railroad.

Length of road, . .   144.0 miles,   4,225,435 00

   Cost of   . .   3,025.6 miles, $173,457,057 09

Average cost per mile, including equipment, . $57,341 17

We will hereafter discuss fully the value of the trade brought to and taken from Pittsburg for the Pennsylvania Railroad by these lines, but we desire now to learn—

First.—What are the prospects for the future of these lines?

Second.—At what figure may we place the liability of the Pennsylvania Railroad Company for them?

First, then, the prospects of these lines of railroad for the future. The building of railroads in the West is acknowledged to have gone beyond the ability of the country to make them profitable.

The competition of the trunk lines from east to west has cut down prices of transportation and travel below the point of profit. For some of the direct lines in the near West there has been sufficient trade and travel to have paid at fair rates the interest on their funded debt, and on many of them a dividend on the stock; but roads have been carried to the extreme verge of population, and, to enable the producers at these far points to send their produce to market, prices have been fixed by competition too low to pay the cost of carriage. The stockholders of the new roads holding land grants, and the many roads built on speculation, desire to attract settlers on their lines, and therefore favor the continuance of these low rates until they can dispose of their lands or get rid of their investments.

The most of these land grants to railways have been unwisely given by Congress, and have drawn the people far beyond the point where the farmer can be repaid for his labor by the money value of his products and the railway for its transportation. One or the other or both must go down. There is a limit at which transportation can be done, viz., paying the absolute cost of the work without reference to bonds or stock, and there is a minimum price which the farmer must get for his produce to give him the means of existence. With these two limits fixed, it would not be difficult to define the extreme limit of expense-paying production. If the speculators who build these railways were the only losers of money, and the farmer who exiles himself and his family from many of the benefits of civilized life was the only sufferer, we might say, let them do as they please, for the limit of injury would be quickly reached. But the speculator pushes off his worthless stocks and bonds on innocent and confiding persons, thereby inflicting wide-spread harm, and seriously affecting the character and credit of the nation, while the farmer inflicts an irreparable wrong on his children. In this whole subject there is a question of morals involved.

It is just these facts that the people in the West should consider. So great has been the infatuation of the public mind in the East, as to the value of the western trade, that they have thought there was no limit to the ability to produce and the power to transport profitably the staple productions of the West eastward to the Atlantic. The experience of the Pennsylvania Railroad Company, as we shall hereafter show, pricks the bubble of the value of the western trade and travel to the trunk lines. If these statements are true, what then? Plainly two things—

1. The far West must cease to produce grain, depending on the East and Europe for their market. Population must not go beyond the point where the producer and transporter can be both paid for their labor.

2. To secure the largest and freest development of the rich fields of the West, the consumer must be brought near to the farmer; which simply means—the manufacturer and the grain-grower must be close together. The less need of transportation the better, as between the producer and consumer. The saving of this cost of transportation is just so much added to the value of the products of the farmer and so much added to the profits of the manufacturer. The valleys of the Ohio and Mississippi must become the great workshop of this country. This realized, any demand from abroad for the cereals of the West would be met by a price which would compensate the farmer for his labor and capital, and the railroad company as the carrier.

The western railways will not become profitable investments until this end is reached. They cannot be made to pay at any thing like the through rates they have received during the past few years. It would certainly seem reasonable to expect that the able men in charge of our general railway system would not permit the mere question of rivalry to prevail any longer and prevent them from fixing paying rates from east to west and from west to east. They should see that by their own impolitic course they are but extending the evil of a population reaching beyond the point where a living can be made by farming.

If they establish paying rates it will tend to centralize population, develop towns and cities, and create in place of destroying wealth, and the western people will soon learn the lesson that their produce can no longer be carried below cost, nor will the few who travel from west to east and back again be transported in Pullman cars at the cost of the share or bond holder.

Or look at this question from another point of view.

The recent war raised the price of produce to a very profitable figure, and thereby stimulated the building of railways in the West. The success of those lines built and in use during the war, the profits in farming, and the springing up of thriving towns, seemed to prove that such results would continue to the limit of the ability to build railways. But since the war, prices have been gradually decreasing: a succession of large crops caused by labor returning measurably to its old channels, favorable seasons, and peace in Europe, have so reduced prices that, to meet this reduction, the railways have cut down their tariffs to the point where transportation has become less profitable. Already millions of dollars of capital invested in western railways which, a few years ago, were thought to be securely invested, have been sunk, and the startling problem is, how much further will this go, and how long will it continue? The freight charges over railroads depending on the carriage of the products of the farm cannot go much lower. The stock of some of such roads is sunk, and any further reduction in rates will destroy the capacity of these roads to pay the interest on their funded debt, and bring them down to absolute cost of transportation.

It is also well to note, as having an important bearing on this question, that the area of grain-producing land is increasing, in the great producing countries of the world, while the ability to consume does not show a proportioned increase. The prospect this year is for another large crop following the one of 1873,—the inevitable result, unless fortuitous circumstances interfere, will be lower prices for grain and meats. We thus have these three facts before us:—

1. That the tendency of prices for the products of the farm is downward;

2. That the cost of transportation cannot be safely reduced below existing rates;

3. That the products of the farm from the far West will not, at the present rates, profitably bear railroad transportation to the East and pay the railroad company a fair price for its carriage, or the farmer a just reward for his labor and capital invested.

With this discouraging outlook into the future, is it strange that we find the western farmers moving in their strength to find out what can be done to drive away the grim figure of poverty which threatens them? That their first attack is on the transporter is natural; he seems to be their nearest enemy, and as they have none of the stocks or bonds of the railroad companies, and the owners are afar off, the foreigner's property is a tempting object of attack, even to destruction. There is in this truth a moral that the stockholders of the Pennsylvania Railroad Company may well learn: that the strength of a railway company in meeting unjust attacks on its property lies more in the fact of the people who use the road having a strong personal interest in it, as stockholders, than in the justice of their cause. And this is the explanation of the condition of things in Wisconsin and Iowa. The same influences may yet meet you in other Western States. But to return from this digression.

The western farmers will soon find, if they succeed in destroying the capital invested in the railways, that this will not relieve them. They must realize the truth of their position and acknowledge the fact that *they have gone too far west.* The farmer of to-day is unlike the farmer of earlier days. He has not his habits of economy and thrift. Many things which are now necessaries to the farmer and his family were unknown to their fathers, or, if known, were considered luxuries. Those who settled the Middle States had the knowledge and ability to feed and clothe their families within themselves, and were, therefore, more independent than the farmer of to-day. Again, we have all been dazzled with the wonderful growth of the West, and, as her cities have arisen in a day, have thought such development could not be without a sound basis to build upon. But as we look closer, we find those cities have grown up and become rich as the home of the middle-man between the producer and the consumer, the manufacturer and the wearer. These men have fixed the prices of, and speculated on, the productions of the farmer, and have heretofore made large profits on the necessaries of life sold to him. It is, to some extent, reproducing the history of every purely agricultural country in the old world, with cities of great wealth, and surrounding millions of producers in great poverty. To the majority of our people all this may read as an exaggerated statement; but a reference to the books of our merchants will prove the truth of our statements.

We again come to the conclusion heretofore arrived at: that the only hope for the western farmer is, either to move eastward and let the capital involved in the roads built to the far West be entirely sunk, or to draw the consumer to his side, save the capital expended in the railways, and thereby secure the benefits already stated. The increase of manufacturing in the States of Ohio, Indiana, Illinois, and Missouri shows that the minds of many have appreciated the necessities of their position. They see that their cities must have some surer basis of wealth and growth than acting simply as middle-men, and that the one tends to poverty, the other to wealth.

For the West to think of depending on England as a market for its produce and as a place to purchase its manufactured goods is suicidal, and not much less to depend on the Middle States and the East for the same character of market and the same source of supply. Your committee have felt authorized thus fully to discuss these points, for in them lies much of the future of the roads you are interested in west of Pittsburg. You cannot look forward to much change in their condition while so much of their business is through and low-priced freight, on which they receive but a *pro rata* of charges between points west and east. Their policy must be to encourage local trade and travel, to offer every inducement for parties to introduce manufacturing and industrial works on their lines, and to let the through business be the surplus products, put into the more concentrated shape of cattle, hogs, &c.

Paradoxical as it may appear, the Pennsylvania Railroad Company will realize more money from its western investments, and more profit on your main line, when you receive less tonnage, because the products of the farm from those roads, for the tonnage that will then be sent eastward, will be of higher value, being labor and food in condensed shape, and necessarily bear a higher and more profitable rate of freight.

Your committee, in their visit to the western roads, made diligent inquiry on this point of local trade. Your Northern or Fort Wayne system is profitable, because it has a large and rapidly increasing local business, making exchanges of ore for coal, iron for cattle and grain, &c., &c., and these within the range or limits of its own roads.

For the Southern system so much cannot be said. By competition, the Little Miami Railroad, which until lately was one of the most successful railways in the country, has been reduced to one of the poorest paying of your lines. Owing to some mismanagement, or the rivalry of its northern competitors, it lost the business of the Cleveland, Columbus and Cincinnati Railway, which furnished more than one-half its total receipts, and caused that company to build a rival line to Cincinnati via Dayton and Springfield. This loss leaves the rental extravagantly high, and the line is a burden on the Pittsburg, Cincinnati and St. Louis Company. The receipts on this line will gradually increase, as it runs through a rich and thickly settled country, and controls the entrance into Cincinnati on the eastern side of the city.

The Columbus, Chicago and Indiana Central also stands at too high a rental for the character of the road and the country through which it passes. There will be improvement on it, but as it, with its Illinois State Line Branch, passes through an almost purely agricultural country, this improvement in earnings will come slowly, and a large portion of the rental will probably be a charge on the Pittsburg, Cincinnati and St. Louis Company for some years to come.

The Jeffersonville, Madison and Indianapolis road has better prospects, and should soon cease to be a debtor road. The Indianapolis and Vincennes road will continue to be a charge for some years, unless the trade from the Cairo and Fulton road can be secured for it, which is not very probable, and the competition at Cairo of the Illinois Central Railroad would destroy any such probabilities. The Indianapolis and St. Louis road will in time pay,—it now clears its interest and has a fair future before it.

The Vandalia Line to St. Louis, as a part of the direct line from New York to St. Louis, will grow rapidly. The new bridge at St. Louis adds greatly to its value; and lastly, *the Pittsburg, Cincinnati and St. Louis Railway*, a part of the main line to St. Louis, Cincinnati, and the South, with the trade that must be thrown upon it by the many roads that join and intersect it, by the valuable coal traffic that originates on its main line, should be able readily to meet all the interest on its funded debt—with a good prospect for very great improvement in its financial results as a whole.

The second point designated above was to see or to estimate, if possible, the extent of the ultimate responsibility of the Pennsylvania Railroad Company for the engagements of the Pittsburg, Cincinnati and St. Louis Railway Company.

Taking the losses of 1873 as a basis, which amounted to	$2,476,143 39
And the General Manager's estimate of value of the betterments as correct, at	1,724,395 51
Would leave a balance of	$751,747 88

as the real loss on that system of roads.

By the statement of loss on the Southern system of roads, you will note there was an aggregate charge of $540,088.57, being for discount on sale of bonds paid by those roads on account of their floating debt, which would reduce the amount of loss in working those roads to $211,649.31.

Now we do not see how the Pittsburg, Cincinnati and St. Louis line can stand under much more bonded indebtedness than it now has, and we therefore think it safe that you should estimate, as a possible future loss on this line of roads, at least $500,000 a year. This limit may be passed, and yet, with fair success in the administration of your Fort Wayne or Northern system under the Pennsylvania Company, the profits there should square the accounts between the two systems, or leave an unimportant balance on one side or the other.

The trade centres in the West reached by your systems of railway are surely enough, and the responsibilities assumed sufficiently great, to satisfy the most ambitious. You can now stop with safety, and your interests will be best taken care of by carefully nursing these western investments; limiting their expansion or extension, unless the local demands require it, and hoping for the time when, by some arrangement, it will not be necessary for you to employ so much capital in holding these roads.

It is but just to say, that at the time these contracts were made, the prices for freight were much higher than in 1873. If the same prices had been received in 1873 as existed when they were made, the result would have been much more favorable. It was also fair to presume at the time the contracts were made, that the present low prices were not thought possible, or that managers of railroads would, through mere rivalry, so depreciate their own property.

The same principle that has led your Company into unwise investments has drawn prudent men in their private affairs to greater proportionate expansion,—the history of trade is full of warning on this point.

2. Value of the Competitive Passenger Travel and Freight Received from and Sent to the Western Lines over the Pennsylvania Railroad—Main Line.

In former parts of this report, we promised a discussion of this important question. We were led to examine it the more thoroughly from the prominent position which "western trade and travel" have occupied in the public estimation for so many years.

In the early years of our national existence, the passage of the mountains was accomplished by the turnpike which united the East and the West. Philadelphia—at that time the great commercial city of the new nation—commanded the best means of access to the West, and profited accordingly. Soon New York entered upon the construction of her great canal from Albany to Buffalo, and Pennsylvania, not to be outdone, followed with her mixed system of canal and portage railway from Columbia to Pittsburg. Virginia attempted the same in her James River and Kanawha Canal, but failed to complete it. Millions of dollars were expended in this effort to unite the East and the West.

The introduction of the railway, with the advantage of the speedy locomotive over the weary horse that slowly tugged at the canal-boat, soon produced a new competitor; and as the turnpike gave way to the canal as a cheaper medium of transportation, so the canal gave way to the locomotive, in illustration of the adage that "time is money,"—and a very large amount of money was expended in the effort to build the New York Central, the New York and Erie, and the Baltimore and Ohio Railroads.

Your line came in at a later period, though completed through to Pittsburg before the Baltimore and Ohio Railroad reached Wheeling. With the completion of these lines began the strong competition for this great prize—"the western trade and travel," and the parties interested in the New York Central Railroad Company entered into the struggle for the control of the western lines. The New York and Erie and the Atlantic and Great Western Railroads, after severe struggles, penetrated the West. The Baltimore and Ohio Railroad Company also built her lines to the Ohio, and, besides, made investments north of that river. The Pennsylvania Railroad Company, from the causes heretofore stated, in order to protect itself, was drawn into investments and liabilities heavier than any other line, and being so much involved, felt it to be its true policy to perfect its connections with the great commercial centres of the West, as has been heretofore sketched.

We will now endeavor to ascertain the value to the shareholders of the Pennsylvania Railroad Company of all these efforts.

The traffic that comes east bears the lowest tariff, as is well stated in the last annual report:—" A close examination of the accounts of this Company will show that its charges for freight upon agricultural products scarcely bear the expenses of transportation, and on many items the charges for transportation are below the actual cost." And the competition of the trunk lines has been so close as to reduce materially the profit of the transportation of the valuable articles which the sale of these products enables the merchants and the farmers to purchase in the East for consumption at home.

Now let us ascertain the value of this trade and travel to the Pennsylvania Railroad Company in 1873. The through tonnage coming from Philadelphia and Baltimore, and destined to points west of Pittsburg, and that sent East from the West through Pittsburg, in the year 1873, amounted to—

			Mileage.
Through east,	873,795 tons, yielding	$3,464,690 51	312,362,336
Through west,	319,661 " "	1,111,816 50	114,475,403
	1,193,456	$4,576,507 01	426,837,739

The through freight earnings were	$4,576,507 01
Local freight earnings were	15,032,048 06
Total freight earnings,	$19,608,555 07

The total mileage of tons of freight over the road was . . . . . 1,384,831,970 miles.

Which is equal to passing over the whole road (three hundred and fifty-six miles) of . . . . . 3,890,000 tons.
The through freight (three hundred and fifty-six miles) was . . . . 1,193,456 "

Leaving the local freight equivalent to 2,696,544 tons over the whole line, showing that the through freight was thirty-one per cent. of the whole average over the road.

The table above shows that the receipts for—

Through freight eastward averaged per ton per mile, ...0111 cents.
Through freight westward averaged per ton per mile, ...0097 "
The average through freight earnings would be .0107 "

If the expenses of conducting transportation in 1873 cost, per ton per mile, .0857 cents, it would be fair to place the cost of the through freight per ton per mile at .0070 cents.

The profit on the through freight would then be
On 1,193,456 tons, at .0107—.0070=.0037=$1,588,642 84

Let us now examine the passenger account.

	First Class.	Emigrant.
Number of passengers delivered to connecting lines in Pittsburg, ...	79,296	37,445
Received from connecting lines in Pittsburg, ...	79,017	2,110
	158,313	39,555

The average receipt of through passengers per mile was . . . . 2.36 cents.

The average expense of carrying through passengers on account of speed, heavy cars, &c., was equal to at least the average cost as given in the expenses for 1873, which was, per mile, 2.01 cents.

Showing profit per passenger per mile of .0035, or three mills and one-half.

This, for 158,313 passengers, would give a profit of, at .0035 cents per mile, . . $197,258 00

The profit on freight carried was . . . 1,588,642 84

Showing total profit on through passenger and freight traffic, ... $1,785,900 84

It is curious to note that the through freight and through passengers are very nearly equal to one-third the total amount of freight and number of passengers passing over the whole length of your road.

Now the capital employed in your main line in 1873 was $53,360,456.03, and to charge the through business with one-third of this capital would give $17,786,818.68, on which it would show a profit of $1,785,900.84, or a fraction under ten per cent. per annum.

This profit is to be considered in connection with the investments of money made, the value of the guarantees given on these western roads, the effect the transportation of this western business has on the cost of the general movement of traffic and passengers on the main line, and the real amount of business the control of these roads gives you.

But whether or not these western roads pay financially to your main line, it is true that the Pennsylvania Railroad was built to bring trade and travel through the State of

Pennsylvania to the city of Philadelphia, which it undoubtedly has done, and, if necessary, reasonable sacrifice of some profit should be made for these objects.

Interests South of Cairo.

We cannot omit to mention with regret that a large interest of $1,300,000 is held by the Pennsylvania Company, originally taken by the Pennsylvania Railroad Company, in the line of railroad from opposite Cairo to New Orleans. The principle upon which this investment was made is, in our judgment, indefensible. We are glad to add that recently the Company has received large returns from this investment and still controls, for commercial purposes, the whole line of railroad from New Orleans to Cairo without cost.

Interests South of Baltimore.

This interest is divided into several lines—

1. The Baltimore and Potomac Railroad Company.

2. The Alexandria and Fredericksburg Railroad Company.

3. Southern Security Company.

4. Danville and Atlanta Lines.

The Baltimore and Potomac Railroad extends from Baltimore to Pope's creek, seventy-three and one-tenth miles, with a branch of nineteen and two-tenths miles to Washington, making a single-track railway ninety-two and three-tenths miles long, with a tunnel through part of the city of Baltimore, which is represented by a cost of $9,888,736 (or over $107,000 per mile, including tunnel),—consisting of stock $3,503,900, bonds $4,500,000, and floating debt $1,884,836.

The bonds are guaranteed by the Northern Central and Pennsylvania Railroad Companies, and therefore will always be a safe investment.

The object in constructing this road was three-fold: first, to make a southern extension for the Northern Central Railway to the city of Washington; second, a more perfect connection with your New York lines; and, third, to furnish a route for the southern travel from the roads of the Southern Security Company northward and eastward.

The drawback to this whole scheme is that all these three inducements are not enough to make it pay much more than the cost of working it and keeping up and improving the line, as should always be done, without adding to construction account. You must therefore estimate a yearly charge on your profit and loss account of one-half the amount of the interest on the bonds of this company.

We regret, with this investment, to add those in the

Alexandria and Fredericksburg Railway stock,	$31,600 00
Alexandria and Washington Railway stock, .	63,724 00
Southern Railway Security Company, . .	783,734 33
Richmond and Danville Railroad stock, .	600,000 00
Notes of the Richmond and Danville, bonds of the Atlanta Railroad and Richmond and Atlanta Air-Line, with collateral of $3,205,691.42, ...	1,164,997 00
Western Railroad of Alabama stock, . .	60,000 00
Amounting in all to . . .	$2,704,065 33

which, though charged off to the profit and loss account of 1873, yet reveals an illegitimate direction given to the funds and credit of the Pennsylvania Railroad Company. which cannot be approved. The securities above named, with others in the profit and loss account, we have valued at $1,000,000, with not much prospect of improvement.

We are glad to add that your Company is now in no way liable for any guarantees, leases, or otherwise on account of any railroad south of Washington.

4. *The Eastern Group.*

We now come to the consideration of the lines of railway and canal under your control and owned by you east of Pittsburg and Erie. This may be called the Eastern or Pennsylvania system, and consists of seven divisions, viz.:—

	Miles.
1. The Allegheny Valley Railroad Division,	446
2. The Philadelphia and Erie Railroad Division,	288
3. The Northern Central Railway Division,	309
4. The Pennsylvania Canal Company Division,	347
5. The United Railroads of New Jersey Division,	344
6. The Delaware and Raritan Canal Division,	61
7. The Pennsylvania Railroad Division,	1021
Total miles railway,	2408
Total miles canal,	408

As perhaps properly connected with this system, we name—

8. The Pittsburg, Virginia and Charleston Railroad. This road is to extend from South Pittsburg up the Monongahela valley to Charleston. It is built and was opened in 1873 to Monongahela City, a distance of thirty miles. The object of this line, in addition to developing the local trade of the valley, is to draw its trade and travel to Pittsburg, there meeting your several lines east and west, but more especially to open, by means of a short branch from this road, a connection with your main line near Brinton's Station. This piece of road will be valuable, as it will afford the means of passing through freight between your main line and the Pittsburg, Cincinnati and St. Louis Road, without going through the city of Pittsburg proper.

9. The Columbia and Port Deposit Railroad, a branch about forty miles long, between Columbia and Port Deposit, partially graded, and when finished it will make a connection with the Philadelphia, Wilmington and Baltimore Railroad at Perryville, and thus open new markets for the distribution of the coal of the Susquehanna valley.

1. The Allegheny Valley Railroad Division.

	Miles.
This division consists of the Allegheny Valley Railroad proper, extending from Pittsburg to Oil City,	132
The Low-Grade Extension, ... 110	
Other branches, ... 37	
	147
The Oil Creek and Allegheny River Railroad, .	123
The Buffalo, Corry and Pittsburg Railroad, .	44
Total, ...	446

This road passes through one of the most valuable freight-producing valleys in the State, abounding in coal, iron, oil, timber, and other products; its branches connect with the Philadelphia and Erie, Atlantic and Great Western, and Lake Shore Railroads on the north, the Philadelphia and Erie on the east, by means of the "Low-Grade Line," and the Pennsylvania Railroad on the south. Thus located, commanding such immense tonnage, prudent management should have made it profitable to its owners. The history of its recent financial troubles we need not repeat, but congratulate all parties interested in the prospect of their being removed. It will take years of patient labor and continued confidence in the ultimate result by its stockholders before the effect of the errors of judgment committed can be overcome, and their stock be again worth what it has been.

These lines have advantages which in time will largely increase their traffic, and may make some of the branches profitable, but which for a time will entail an annual expense.

It is thought by some of your officers that this road will be able to pay the interest, as it becomes due, on the bonds of the "Low-Grade Line." These bonds are endorsed, interest and principal, by the Pennsylvania Railroad Company, and are therefore a good security to the holders.

2. The Philadelphia and Erie Railroad Division.

So fully have your directors reported as to the condition and prospects of this road, that little more is left for us to add. The unfortunate location of the road between Driftwood and Warren—with its two summits of two thousand and six feet and one thousand six hundred and eighty-two feet to overcome, and lying north of the line of abundant coal and heavy timber—causes it to traverse a country moderately timbered, and which, when cut off, leaves an unproductive slate soil. The result will be that, in a few years, the local trade and travel will have a tendency to decrease rather than to increase.

The competition of other roads along most of its line prevents its receiving fair rates for its local business, while its through business has close competition with water and rail lines to the east and west. The fears of many early interested in this line seem to be realized, that so long a line of rail cannot successfully compete with the water and rail lines to New York. Much more has been expected from the completion of the "Low-Grade Line" than seems warranted. Let us look at it:—The trade coming to or going from your line over that road would use one hundred and twenty miles of the track of the Philadelphia and Erie Railroad.

The leading reasons for building the "Low-Grade Line" we understand to be—

1. A strategic movement to control the valley of the Bennett's Branch at the lowest summit of the mountains between the east and the west in Pennsylvania.

2. The making a good connection with the oil regions for transportation of oil eastward.

3. The development of the minerals on its lines and the manufacture of its timber into lumber.

4. The carrying fourth class freight at slow speed, at very low rates, from west to east.

The first three points are tenable, though it is questionable whether the strategic advantages are worth the cost, or whether the oil cannot be carried by way of the Western Pennsylvania Railroad and your main line at really as low rates and much quicker than by the "Low-Grade Road." There certainly is not enough to be gained, by whatever advantage the "Low-Grade Line" might have in this respect, to warrant its being built at a cost of near $12,900,000, or over $117,000 per mile.

As to the fourth argument, we think it defective for three reasons—

1. The Pennsylvania Railroad Company would lose by sending freight from Pittsburg east by that line. If its main line should be overloaded, it would be wiser to enlarge its capacity than to turn away the business on to another road.

2. The question whether freight shippers would regard the small saving in charges as an equivalent to loss in time. The saving in time for one hundred and ten miles would not be much, and when it reaches the Philadelphia and Erie Road, slow speed could only be used on about seventy miles of that road; so that the whole distance on which slow speed could be used would be one hundred and eighty miles, which could not make a difference of over ten hours in time, which is not worth much reduction in rates.

3. The working a line at slow speed practically limits the capacity of the line, and involves large additional expenditure of motive power and cars.

We cannot, therefore, look forward to any large increase of traffic from this source; and should there be a large tonnage on the principle of low rates and slow speed, it would probably be years before it is realized, and when it does come will be of little pecuniary gain to that road.

The most we can hope from the Philadelphia and Erie Railroad is, that it will earn enough to pay the interest on its funded debt and the Pennsylvania Railroad Company for the interest on its equipment.

According to the report of your directors of March 11th, 1873, the Philadelphia and Erie Railroad, with a single track, represents a cost per mile of $75,744, while the Pennsylvania Railroad, with two tracks, represents but $71,999 per mile; and that since 1869, while the increase in gross receipts has been but $17\frac{7}{10}$ per cent., the increase in bonded debt and preferred stock has been $39\frac{6}{10}$ per cent. These two facts furnish little ground for hope in the future that more will ever be realized than enough to satisfy the claims of the Pennsylvania Railroad Company for working the road and for advances already made to cover the deficiency of net receipts.

3. The Northern Central Railway.

	Miles.
Main line from Baltimore to Sunbury,	138
Shamokin Valley and Pottsville Railroad,	28
Elmira and Williamsport Railroad, held by lease,	78
Chemung Railroad,*	18
Elmira, Jefferson and Canandaigua Railroad,*	47
Total,	309

*These roads are held by the Northern Central Railway Company, owning four thousand seven hundred and six of the five thousand shares of the Chemung Railroad, and fourteen thousand and twenty-two shares of the fifteen thousand two hundred shares of the Elmira, Jefferson and Canandaigua Railroad.

The importance of this line of road will be appreciated when you trace its connections. At Baltimore it connects with the Baltimore and Potomac Railroad to Washington and the South, passes north through a beautiful and rich country to Harrisburg, where it reaches your main line and makes connection with the Cumberland Valley Railroad and the system of railroads under control of the Reading Railroad Company, and thence to Sunbury, having also valuable branches by rail to the Lykens valley coal mines, the Trevorton mines, and by the Shamokin Valley Railroad to the fine coals of that valley, and to a large body of coal land owned by that company near Shamokin.

At Williamsport it takes control of the Elmira and Williamsport Railroad to Elmira, and thence, by the Elmira and Canandaigua Railroad, secures a market in the centre of the State of New York and in the cities of Rochester and Buffalo for anthracite coal, and also makes valuable connections with the New York and Erie and New York Central Railroad lines.

The natural division of this line would be to work the road from Harrisburg to Baltimore as a branch to your main line, and to place the Shamokin Valley Railroad, with the line to Buffalo (through Elmira), under the Philadelphia and Erie Railroad management. It is to be regretted that this course was not adopted as soon as you acquired the lease of the Philadelphia and Erie Railroad. The many economic advantages of this plan are apparent, and it is to a limited extent so managed at this time.

The Northern Central Railway is not only a valuable feeder to and distributor of products taken from your road to local points on either road and to the West, but it has a large local trade, and is one of the great coal avenues from the mines to the Atlantic coast.

The growing local trade of this line between Buffalo and Baltimore, with the through trade thrown on it by your road, requires largely increased facilities at its terminus in Baltimore,—that city having built the Union Railroad to connect the Northern Central Railway with the bay, making a complete line to tide-water. These facilities are required to handle cheaply the coal, lumber, grain, live stock, oil, &c. that comes over that line. The financial inability of the Northern Central Railway Company to complete its terminal improvements and stock its road, causes it, naturally, to look for aid to its main stockholder, who is so largely interested, not only as a stockholder, but also as a gainer by these improvements in the traffic it will bring to its main line.

The advantages arising from the natural alliances and economic workings of the mixed lines of the Northern Central Railway above suggested—the absolute value of these lines to your main line—and the financial inability of the Northern Central Company to develop and take care of its growing trade—plainly indicate that a just lease of that road or other satisfactory arrangement would be advantageous to the interests of stockholders in both companies.

4. *The Pennsylvania Canal Division.*

The ownership and control of the Canal property in Pennsylvania fell to your Company in the purchase of the public works throughout the State. The unjust discrimination made by the State of Pennsylvania in the tonnage tax, rendered it necessary for the Company to pave the way to its abrogation, as well as to secure the railroad from Philadelphia to Columbia by purchase. This took place in 1857, and consisted of the railroad from Philadelphia to Columbia, and the canals extending thence by the Juniata to Pittsburg, with the Portage Railroad and other appurtenances. The price paid was $7,500,000, of which $1,000,000 was apportioned upon the Company's books as the value of the canals purchased. The Portage road and the Pittsburg Division of the canal were abandoned. The portion of the canal line retained extends from Columbia to Hollidaysburg, about one hundred and seventy-three miles.

In 1867 this canal interest was organized as an independent corporation, with the corporate title of the Pennsylvania Canal Company, with a capital stock of $2,750,000, which represented the $1,000,000 originally paid the State, with the interest thereon and expenditures for enlargement of the canal after it came into the possession of your Company. In 1867 the majority of the stock of the West Branch and Susquehanna Canal, extending from Clark's Ferry to Farrandsville, on the West Branch, a distance of one hundred and twenty-three miles, was purchased with the bonds of the Pennsylvania Canal Company, and afterwards, as its indebtedness matured or approached maturity, it was taken up in exchange for canal bonds having forty years to run. This enabled your Company to reach the lumber regions on the West Branch; and in order to have access to the anthracite coal fields, the Pennsylvania Canal Company, in 1869, merged with the Wyoming Valley Canal, by the exchange of an equal number of shares of its stock —exchanging its forty-year bonds at par for the mortgage bonds of the Wyoming Company, then about maturing, amounting to $600,000. In 1872, for the purpose of giving direct access by water to the Lykens Valley coal fields, there was purchased most of the stock and all of the indebtedness of the Wiconisco Canal, extending from Clark's Ferry to Millersburg, for one thousand nine hundred and eighty-two shares of Pennsylvania Canal stock. Afterwards the West Branch and Wiconisco Canals were sold under judgment and purchased by the Pennsylvania Canal Company, which thus became the absolute owner of all these several canals, embracing altogether about three hundred and sixty miles. These canals having become much deteriorated, and their capacity reduced, while great improvements had taken place in the rail lines, it was decided to enlarge and improve the main line, extending from Columbia to Wilkesbarre, and procure a stock of boats, in order to insure regular transportation. This policy having been determined upon, the whole earnings of the canal, in excess of the ordinary expenditures and interest, were applied to the purpose, down to the end of 1873, when a stock of one hundred and eighty-four boats had been acquired and the enlargement of the main line completed. This enlargement consisted in widening and deepening the canal, doubling the length of the locks, and renewing all important structures on the line,—using durable materials, and making them of a permanent character. The capacity of the lockage was increased from eighty to two hundred and sixty gross tons; the cost of shipment from Wilkesbarre to Havre de Grace was reduced from two dollars and twenty-five cents to one dollar per gross ton, and from eleven and twenty-five-one-hundredths mills to five mills per gross ton per mile. Without this improvement it is now evident that the canals would have been abandoned or sustained serious and constant losses. The history of water navigation has established one fact beyond dispute, that to compete with the present low rates of freight on railroads, boats should be constructed to carry not less than two hundred and fifty tons gross. The nearer this minimum tonnage is attained or exceeded, the more certainty is there of a return. In enlarging the main lines of canals the tonnage has been increased to about two hundred and sixty to two hundred and eighty tons. It is to be regretted that the minimum capacity was not made three hundred tons. The whole expenditure on enlargement account, on the 31st December, was $1,983,499,—about $13,223 per mile,—which compares favorably with the expenditures of other canals for like purposes. It is claimed by the officers of the canal that the whole cost of these improvements was earned from the line during the progress of the work.

From sources of information at its disposal, your committee is led to believe that the earnings of the canals will pay the working expenses, the interest on the funded debt, and lay by a sufficient sum to meet the principal at maturity.

These canals in other hands, at the present reduced prices of transportation, might have been used to the disadvantage of your Company.

Nothing has been done towards the enlargement of the Juniata division, which extends to the bituminous regions, that being postponed until the results of the present work are fully ascertained.

5. United Railroads of New Jersey.

These lines, so lately brought under your charge, will prove this year the wisdom of the lease. The causes of the losses in working them in 1871, 1872, and 1873 have been clearly stated in the reports of the directors: 1874 will demonstrate their ability to pay all charges, and probably yield hereafter a surplus, which, in time, will largely provide for necessary enlargements, additions, or betterments.

The United Railroads of New Jersey Division.

These lines embrace the following railroads:—

	Miles.
Mantua to New York,	89
Camden to South Amboy,	61
Princeton Branch,	3
Rocky Hill and Kingston Railroad,	6
Millstone and New Brunswick Railroad,	7
Perth Amboy and Woodbridge Railroad,	7
Monmouth Junction to Jamesburg,	6
Pemberton and Hightstown Railroad,	25
Camden and Burlington County Railroad,	25
Columbus, Kinkora and Springfield Railroad,	14
Burlington and Mount Holly Railroad,	7
Medford Branch,	7
Vincentown Branch,	3
Mercer and Somerset Railroad,*	5
Frankford and Holmesburg Railroad,	5
Bordentown to Trenton,	6
	276

* Seventeen miles additional have been opened in 1874.

Belvidere Division.

	Miles.
Belvidere Delaware Railroad,	68
Flemington Branch,	12
	80
	356

The importance of the control of the United Railroads of New Jersey with the Belvidere Division and the Raritan Canal will not now be questioned, for it secured—

1. A continuous line of railroad between the city of New York and the West under one control.

2. The use of the unrivaled terminal advantages at the city of New York, Jersey City, and South Amboy.

3. The key of the line of southern travel to Baltimore and Washington.

4. The ability to place the products of the mine and the farm on tide-water, at the least expense, nearest to the centre of shipment and consumption.

5. The power to fix through rates.

6. The control of a line of railroads and canal that must continually increase in value and profit.

These points are of immense value to the Pennsylvania Railroad Company, and by this lease many serious impediments to your success were removed, among which we note—

The Terminal Difficulties.

1. The United Companies would not furnish the necessary terminal facilities at Jersey City and South Amboy to handle the freight you were prepared to send, and receive a *pro rata* freight, and it seemed impossible to make any arrangement by which the Pennsylvania Railroad Company could furnish part of the cost of such terminal facilities and yet be itself secured.

2. Any written contract between the companies for conducting the business would have been subject to constant change and have given rise to continual misunderstandings.

3. The Pennsylvania Railroad Company could not have relied on a contract which would warrant its making the necessary outlays to meet the trade.

4. It could not have confined the United Companies to its policy of making the working of that company's roads and canal entirely subsidiary to the interests of the Pennsylvania Railroad Company.

These and other considerations were, doubtless, present in the minds of your directors before making the lease. They were also clear in their judgment as to the imperative necessity that the Pennsylvania Railroad should have a connection, by rail, with the city and bay of New York; and it became a simple question with your Company whether to lease the roads already built or to build a road to meet the demand arising from the largely increasing trade on your own lines seeking an eastern market.

It was to the interest of both parties that a lease should be made, and though at the time of its execution it seemed unfavorable to your Company, yet, as the needed improvements are made and come into use, the advantages of the lease are more clearly seen and its wisdom realized.

These improvements involve—

1. A total change in the location of the machine and repair shops of the New Jersey Company. They must now be located and worked in harmony with those of your main line. Extensive and costly shops are partly built on the Hackensack meadows, four miles from Jersey City, (where your Company owns in its own right one hundred acres, in addition to thirty acres owned by the United Companies,) and smaller shops must be built for the southern lines at Camden, where you have fifty acres with a river front.

2. There has been laid, and must continue to be, a large extent of sidings, not only along the line of the road, but in the yards at Amboy, Hackensack, and Jersey City, and the gradual completion of a system of third and fourth tracks,

which has been adopted for the New York Division, of which thirty-four miles were laid in 1873.

3. The improvements at South Amboy, where the Company owns four hundred and thirty-three acres, with a water front of six thousand feet, have been very great, and have involved heavy expense. They include the entire reconstruction and enlargement of the yard; the laying in 1873 of twenty miles of double track and sidings; the building of inland storage bins for coal (with a capacity of thirty thousand tons, making the total stocking capacity one hundred and seventy thousand tons), to be filled when trade is dull, thereby employing the equipment of the road continually, and enabling this line to carry to market during the year a larger tonnage than they otherwise could do, and the building of a coal wharf having a water frontage of three thousand three hundred and thirty feet. The total shipping frontage is now seven thousand four hundred and ninety feet, with a transshipping capacity of two million tons per annum. There has been expended up to June 1st, 1874, on account of needed improvements at Amboy, $563,449.40.

4. The Harsimus Cove property has a frontage on the North river of one thousand five hundred and eighty feet, of which one thousand three hundred has a depth of three thousand one hundred and forty feet, and the remaining two hundred and eighty feet a depth of one thousand four hundred feet from the warden's line,—the whole containing an area of seventy-five acres, and with the necessary wharves built will give a wharf frontage of three miles. To reach this property a temporary railroad has been constructed, which will answer the purpose until the coming fall, when a permanent connection will be made from the Bergen Cut to the Cove. There has been expended on this connection up to June 1st, 1874, $568,995.26, of which $309,049.52 was for

right of way and other appurtenant property, leaving $259,945.74 for construction.

The improvement at the Cove consists of a large pier two thousand two hundred feet long and three hundred and twenty feet wide, which is mainly used by the Central Stock-Yard and Transit Company for its *abattoir* purposes and as a stock-yard. The Pennsylvania Railroad Company advanced them $300,000, which is secured by a mortgage on the improvements. The stock-yard company also have at Hackensack a hog *abattoir* of very large proportions. The completeness and extent of this company's operations will give you some idea what facilities are required to furnish beef, mutton, and pork to a great city like New York, and of the great value it is to your line of road to have such vast structures located on your property, giving you thereby more than an equal chance in drawing the great cattle trade (since the completion of the bridge over the Mississippi river at St. Louis) over your main lines from St. Louis, Cincinnati, Chicago, and other points to New York.

There is also built on this property another wharf, on which has been erected a freight shed one thousand feet long by one hundred and twenty feet wide, a covered pier, for shipping grain, five hundred feet long by forty-two feet wide, and two car ferry bridges. In and about these improvements five miles of track are laid. There is also room for another pier of equal size to those already built.

It is in contemplation to erect a large elevator and warehouse for storage purposes on this property, which will add largely to the facilities of handling the grain and other traffic that may come to New York over your road, and save in the cost of handling the same.

The total amount charged to cost of Harsimus Cove improvements to June 1st, 1874, is $726,474.80.

The passenger station at the Jersey City ferry has been

rebuilt, giving an additional steamboat dock for the two ferries to the city of New York, and convenient waiting and office rooms, all built on a substantial and very economical plan. There are twenty-two acres of ground connected with the ferry terminus.

5. The freight stations at Piers Nos. 1, 2, 4, 5, 16, 38, and 39, in New York City, are very complete and well adapted for their work. The portage of freight in cars across the North river to these docks proves to be the cheapest method of reaching the centre of trade of a great city like New York. There is a saving of time in reaching the depots; it furnishes more readily points of access to the trade; and saves greatly in the cost of reaching such depots, and in the cost of land and buildings for the same.

This sketch will give some idea of the great improvements that have been made since you have had charge of these lines. We would not have you to think that these improvements are complete or sufficient for any term of years. If we are correct in our views of the inevitable increase of the cattle and of the general trade going over your lines to New York, you must estimate a yearly outlay of money to furnish the necessary enlargements to meet it.

But we look forward to much more extended improvements on your property at Amboy; and it is fortunate that you own the necessary land and river front at that place.

The future demand for hard and soft coals from the city of New York and its adjacent cities—from the country north of it and the entire east—must, in time, amount to a tonnage which, should we now express it in figures, would make us appear too sanguine.

Your control over the valuable anthracites of the Susquehanna, and your relations with shippers from the Lehigh and Wilkesbarre regions, will enable you to fill your share of the demand for hard coal on equal terms with the other great roads. But in the supply of the soft coals you have a decided advantage. Take the gas coals of Westmoreland, the soft coals of the Allegheny mountains—which you control by your main line and branches for many miles—the coals from the Broad Top and from the Cumberland region, the cannel and other valuable coals from the Bennett's Branch Railroad, and then, in addition, with a direct line of railroad having (for the greater part of the distance) a descending grade, and you can place every variety and quality of soft coal at Amboy at a profitable rate to you, and thereby enable shippers by your road to secure the market. We leave you to judge how great will be the demand: only bear in mind that an increased tonnage will require increased facilities.

We notice the passenger travel over this line. A railroad connecting two such cities as New York and Philadelphia alone would afford a profit; but, in addition, this is the line over which all northern and southern travel must pass, and much between the East and West. This, with your rapidly increasing local business, will furnish a constantly increasing passenger travel, which, from the location of the road, can always be made profitable.

Collecting these facts as to traffic and travel, the future of your responsibility as to the lease of this line of railroads need not give you any anxiety. The lines will pay both directly and indirectly very largely to the Pennsylvania Railroad Company. Some of the branches connected with this road are not profitable, but all add to the profit of the two main lines from Philadelphia to Jersey City, and from Camden to Amboy.

6. *The Delaware and Raritan Canal*

Is a very valuable and important water connection between Philadelphia and New York. The result of the management since it came into your hands has been very satisfactory, not in increased tonnage, but in net profits. An examination of the figures of the company presents the following facts:—

The aggregate tonnage of the canal was in 1871, 2,990,095.
The aggregate tonnage of the canal was in 1872, 2,837,532.
The aggregate tonnage of the canal was in 1873, 2,754,837.

This reduction of tonnage was due to throwing a considerable amount of freight from the canal upon the railroad, where it was supposed to return larger profits.

An abstract of the expenditures and receipts for the same period may be interesting, and is as follows:—

RECEIPTS.	1871.	1872.	1873.
Gross canal receipts,	$1,045,957 34	$957,551 25	$1,071,102 74
Gross steam towage receipts,	383,636 77	567,053 99	518,997 38
Total,	$1,429,594 11	$1,524,605 24	$1,590,100 12
Deduct drawbacks refunded,	148,857 27	109,448 80	70,108 75
Actual gross receipts,	$1,280,736 84	$1,415,156 44	$1,519,991 37
Actual expenditures, each carried to its appropriate year, without regard to time of payment,	889,381 97	874,527 23	813,212 71
Net profits,	$391,354 87	$540,629 21	$706,778 66

It will be seen from the above figures that whilst the tonnage of 1873 was 82,695 less than in 1872, the net earnings were $166,149.35 greater; and that whilst the tonnage of 1871 was 135,258 greater than in 1873, the net earnings in 1873 over that year were $315,423.79.

The losses in operating all these lines since they came under your control have been—

In 1871 and 1872,	$1,154,527 57
In 1873,	685,689 70
Amounting to	$1,840,217 27

Though these losses have been charged to expense account, they will be repaid and reappear in the shape of profits. Yet the company is subjected to the cost of the use of the money during the intervening time.

The outlays for improvements on this line are, by the terms of the lease, to be met by an issue of shares in the United Companies in the proportion of thirty thousand shares of stock for $4,000,000 expended.

7. *The Pennsylvania Railroad Division.*

This division consists of the following lines:—

	Miles.
Pennsylvania Railroad Main Line,	358
Columbia Bridge,	1
York Branch,	13
Hollidaysburg Branch,	42
Indiana Branch,	19
East Brandywine and Waynesburg Railroad,	18
Bald Eagle Valley Railroad,	52
Mifflin and Centre County Railroad,	13
Sunbury and Lewistown Railroad,	45
Tyrone and Clearfield Railroad,	44
Ebensburg and Cresson Railroad,	11
Western Pennsylvania Railroad,	85
Bedford and Bridgeport Railroad,	51
South West Pennsylvania Railroad,	24
Pennsylvania and Delaware Railroad,	38
Lewisburg, Centre and Spruce Creek Railroad,	11
Danville, Hazleton and Wilkesbarre Railroad,	44
Cumberland Valley Railroad,	152
Total,	1,021

We do not deem it necessary to discuss each of the branches above named,—to most of the stockholders their condition is well known. The York Branch and Columbia Bridge are now consolidated with your Company; the Hollidaysburg Branch, the Bald Eagle Valley, the Tyrone and Clearfield, the Western Pennsylvania, the South West Pennsylvania, and the Cumberland Valley Railroads are all profitable, and most of the other branches will pay the cost of working; but we fail to see the wisdom of the very peculiar contract or lease of the Danville, Hazleton and Wilkesbarre Railroad. This road can scarcely be expected to pay the cost of working, and to invest money in the purchase of coupons is but to obtain a claim that cannot be paid: the company is certainly in default to its bondholders.

A glance at the accompanying map will show you how these roads penetrate rich agricultural valleys, reach valuable coal fields, forests of timber, and mines of iron ore, and make the necessary connections between the valleys of the Juniata and the Susquehanna, the Juniata and the Potomac, and the Conemaugh and the Monongahela rivers. They are valuable feeders, and, on the whole, are of great financial value to your main line.

The Pennsylvania Railroad Main Line.

After treating of so many railroads of varied strength and usefulness, we with pleasure now refer to this grand line of road—this trunk which gives life and support to so many branches, and which, in return, receives strength from them, —affecting not only the welfare of the State of Pennsylvania, but directly promoting the happiness and prosperity of a large portion of the people of this continent.

Look at its geographical position: commencing on the waters of the Delaware and Schuylkill rivers, and by its connection to New York City, on the North river and New York bay, it passes westward through the richest parts of the State of Pennsylvania; reaching by its arms of iron the valleys of the two branches of the Susquehanna river,—passing along the Juniata river to its source,— numerous connections are made both north and south, reaching mines of ore, forests of timber, and beds of coal; crossing the great water-shed between the waters of the Susquehanna and the Ohio, it is laid upon an almost continuous bed of coal until the Ohio river is reached at Pittsburg, and there by other branches reaches the valleys of the Allegheny and Monongahela rivers. A well-built railroad traversing such a densely-populated country, and connecting two cities like Pittsburg and Philadelphia, could not fail to attract a large and profitable traffic.

To come to details, the Pennsylvania Railroad consists of four parts—

1. The line from Harrisburg to Pittsburg.

2. The line from Harrisburg to Dillerville and from Middletown to Columbia (leased for nine hundred and ninety-nine years from January 1st, 1861), and practically owned by the control of its stock.

3. The Columbia Railroad, from Philadelphia to Columbia (purchased from the State).

4. The Delaware Extension line.

In all forming a direct line from Philadelphia to Pittsburg of three hundred and sixty-five miles, including the Delaware Extension of seven miles.

Cost of Main Line.

By referring to the article on the cost of real estate, road, &c., you will find that the real value of your main line, including the Philadelphia and Columbia Railroad, with the present value of its equipment, real estate, &c., amounts to $94,398,483, while it stands charged on your books at $48,571,808; showing a value exceeding your capital account of $45,826,675.

The retaining of low valuations of personal property in times of great prosperity is an evidence of the wisdom and caution of your late distinguished President. In this connection the following important considerations affecting its value, and necessary to be kept in view in placing an estimate on your property:—

1. That the road from Harrisburg to Pittsburg was built for cash, and at a time of exceptionally low wages.

2. That the Philadelphia and Columbia Railroad (the most valuable eighty miles of railroad in the United States) was purchased from the State at what is now proved to have been a very low figure.

3. The lease of the Harrisburg, Portsmouth, Mt. Joy and Lancaster Railroad was obtained on very favorable terms.

And still further, the real estate owned by the Company (much of it purchased at an early date) is worth a large advance on the price paid for it, as appears in the statement above referred to, which shows a substantial basis for the security of your bonds in addition to the value of the road itself, and saves you from great outlay year by year for lands to accommodate your continually increasing traffic.

Now all these different items give your Company a vantage-ground which will always place it beyond any successful or dangerous competition from present or future rivals; for while the cost of other main roads is fully represented by the amount of stock and indebtedness, on all of which interest and dividends must be paid, your road is expected to pay dividends only on a part of its real value.

Terminal Facilities.

We repeat the summary of the estimates of the real estate, buildings, and improvements given in the former article, as follows:—

Philadelphia Division,	$13,319,133 75
Middle Division,	4,866,598 00
Pittsburg Division,	9,679,509 08
Amounting in all to	$27,865,240 83

These investments of capital are mainly in the cities of Philadelphia, Columbia, Harrisburg, Altoona, and Pittsburg. About $22,000,000 has been expended for terminal facilities, machine and repair shops, depots, &c.

To give you a better idea of the extent of these terminal requirements, take the city of Philadelphia, and you have—

1. The freight depot at Thirteenth and Market streets.

2. The freight depot at Fifteenth and Sixteenth and Market streets.

3. The general office in Fourth street, below Walnut.

4. The emigrant depot, No. 116 Market street.

5. The very large depot grounds, with the machine-shops, in West Philadelphia, extending from the Schuylkill

river to near Hestonville, a distance of about six miles, and covering about three hundred and twenty acres.

6. The one hundred and thirty acres of ground at Greenwich.

7. The Washington Avenue elevator, wharves, and buildings.

8. The extension of rail along the Delaware river front, and the new freight station at the foot of Walnut street.

9. The extensive grounds on the Connecting Railroad purchased for a cattle-yard, containing about two hundred acres.

10. We might properly add, as terminal properties, the large investment made, with your assistance, by private capital at Point Breeze and Girard Point.

We are sure we need go no further to satisfy you that the building of the line of a railroad is but the beginning of the cost. We have gone carefully over the long list of real estate owned by the Company, and find it all required for the business of the road, except a few unimportant and two valuable properties, which can now be sold—the necessity for their ownership having ceased. These two are the stock-yard at East Liberty, near Pittsburg, and the freight depot at Thirteenth and Market streets, in the city of Philadelphia.

The Road and its Appurtenances.

We found your road in capital condition, with care and skill everywhere evidenced in its construction. The introduction of steel rails has been a success, for the time had almost arrived when the substitution of some more durable and safer article than the iron rail would become an absolute necessity.

The shops are judiciously located and substantially constructed, with the most approved machinery and all the modern appliances for saving labor. The locomotives are classified, and thereby repairs are lessened in cost and their time for being in the shop shortened.

The car shops are arranged to build and repair cars at the lowest cost, and so far as we were competent to form an opinion, there was that air of adaptation about all the appurtenances to the road, from one end to the other, which impressed us very favorably with the management thereof.

Cost of Working.

As an evidence of the condition of the road, the motive power, the cars, the shops, machinery, and other adjuncts, we point you to the following table, showing the number of engines used, the number of tons of freight moved one mile, with other details, and at the end the cost of or the rate paid per mile for moving freight:—

Pennsylvania Railroad Division.

Year.	Tons Freight Moved.	Tons One Mile.	No. of Freight Engines.	Distributing Engines.	Shifting Engines.	Average Tons Moved one Mile by each Engine, incl. Distributing and Shifting Engines.	Av'ge Mileage of each Fr't Engine incl. Distribut'g Fr't Engines and Shifting Engines.	Rate per Ton per Mile paid for Moving Freight.
								CENTS.
1864	2,764,876	420,627,222	235	18	13	1,581,305	17,448	$1\frac{87}{100}$
1865	2,555,706	420,060,260	232	24	21	1,516,463	17,987	$2\frac{28}{100}$
1866	3,186,359	513,102,181	253	25	27	1,682,302	18,288	$1\frac{82}{100}$
1867	3,709,224	565,657,813	270	22	36	1,724,566	18,611	$1\frac{64}{100}$
1868	4,427,884	675,775,560	278	29	38	1,958,770	19,521	$1\frac{25}{100}$
1869	4,992,025	752,711,312	314	25	52	1,925,093	18,342	$1\frac{20}{100}$
1870	5,427,401	825,979,692	316	26	53	2,091,088	19,526	$1\frac{00}{100}$
1871	6,575,843	1,011,892,207	338	30	58	2,375,334	21,839	$0\frac{87}{100}$
1872	7,844,778	1,190,144,036	401	34	63	2,389,847	22,302	$0\frac{886}{1000}$
1873	9,211,231	1,384,831,970	456	34	77	2,442,384	23,213	$0\frac{857}{1000}$

The figures in the foregoing table corroborate our statement of the economical workings—a result which could only be reached with a high state of perfection in the three great departments of *Maintenance of Way*, *Motive Power, and Maintenance of Cars*.

We call your particular attention to a few points, knowing they will be very satisfactory, viz.:—

In 1864 it required two hundred and sixty-six locomotives (including shifting and distributing engines) to move 420,627,222 tons of freight one mile, giving average tons moved one mile by each engine, ... 1,581,305
In 1873, five hundred and sixty-seven locomotives moved 1,384,831,970 tons one mile, giving average tons moved one mile by each engine, 2,442,384

A gain of 861,079
tons moved one mile, or over fifty-four per cent. increased service of each engine, while the average mileage of each engine was increased from 17,448 miles in 1864 to 23,213 miles in 1873—an increase of thirty-three per cent.; and the average cost of moving one ton one mile was reduced from $1\frac{87}{100}$ cents in 1864 to $0\frac{857}{1000}$ cents in 1873—a decrease of nearly sixty per cent.

The System of Accounts.

While in our examination we necessarily assumed the accuracy of the books, yet we were the better satisfied to do this, as upon examination of the methods adopted, they show that a charge or entry of a day's labor, of the purchase of a keg of nails, or the largest order, goes through such a series of checks and audits as to make fraud almost an impossibility, requiring, as it would, the assent and knowledge of too many persons to make it safe or successful; yet with all these checks the system is simple and easily carried out.

In the various offices on the road the methods of keeping the details of the cost of working the road in the different departments are very complete, and monthly comparisons of cost are made by each branch,—thereby giving a perfect control over the expenditures and insuring economical results.

These systems of accounts and methods of comparing cost are the growth of years,—a cumulative development, year by year, making it more complete.

The Growth of the Business of the Road compared with Increased Capital.

We have thought it would be interesting, instructive, and satisfactory to the shareholders to know what effect the large expenditures on your main line have had in stimulating the business of your road, and have had prepared the tables following.

Comparative Statement, showing Cost of Road, Tons of Freight Moved, Earnings and Expenses, and Percentage of Increase and Decrease from 1864 to 1873, inclusive.

Year.	Cost of Road and Materials on hand.	Percentage of Increase or Decrease compared with year 1864.	Tons One Mile.	Percentage of Increase or Decrease compared with year 1864.	Freight Earnings.	Freight Expenses.	Net Freight Earnings.	Percentage of Increase or Decrease of Net Freight Earnings compared with year 1864.	Earnings per ton per mile.	Expenses per ton per mile.	Net Earnings per ton per mile.
1864	$32,302,271 90	. . .	420,627,222	. . .	$10,361,999 32	$7,868,195 88	$2,493,803 44	. . .	Cts. $2\tfrac{46}{100}$	Cts. $1\tfrac{87}{100}$	Cts. $0\tfrac{59}{100}$
1865	33,271,889 04	$3\tfrac{0.02}{1000}$	420,060,260	$0\tfrac{135}{1000}$	11,193,565 37	9,582,864 79	1,610,700 58	$35\tfrac{41}{100}$	$2\tfrac{66}{100}$	$2\tfrac{28}{100}$	$0\tfrac{38}{100}$
1866	30,392,257 71	$5\tfrac{913}{1000}$	513,102,181	$21\tfrac{99}{100}$	11,709,293 59	9,342,505 57	2,366,788 02	$5\tfrac{09}{100}$	$2\tfrac{28}{100}$	$1\tfrac{82}{100}$	$0\tfrac{46}{100}$
1867	30,189,965 97	$6\tfrac{539}{1000}$	565,657,813	$34\tfrac{48}{100}$	11,832,299 67	8,732,945 73	3,099,353 94	$24\tfrac{28}{100}$	$2\tfrac{09}{100}$	$1\tfrac{54}{100}$	$0\tfrac{55}{100}$
1868	31,171,362 51	$3\tfrac{501}{1000}$	675,775,560	$60\tfrac{66}{100}$	12,882,165 30	8,440,517 65	4,441,647 65	$78\tfrac{10}{100}$	$1\tfrac{91}{100}$	$1\tfrac{25}{100}$	$0\tfrac{66}{100}$
1869	34,292,295 20	$6\tfrac{161}{1000}$	752,711,312	$78\tfrac{95}{100}$	12,932,656 88	9,035,031 47	3,897,625 41	$56\tfrac{29}{100}$	$1\tfrac{72}{100}$	$1\tfrac{20}{100}$	$0\tfrac{52}{100}$
1870	35,595,146 19	$10\tfrac{0.20}{1000}$	825,979,692	$96\tfrac{37}{100}$	12,793,160 47	8,247,797 18	4,545,363 29	$82\tfrac{27}{100}$	$1\tfrac{55}{100}$	$1\tfrac{00}{100}$	$0\tfrac{55}{100}$
1871	36,404,780 03	$12\tfrac{700}{1000}$	1,011,892,207	$140\tfrac{57}{100}$	14,052,304 51	8,846,694 58	5,205,609 93	$108\tfrac{74}{100}$	$1\tfrac{39}{100}$	$0\tfrac{87}{100}$	$0\tfrac{52}{100}$
1872	44,740,893 35	$38\tfrac{538}{1000}$	1,190,144,036	$182\tfrac{94}{100}$	16,856,891 41	10,546,491 64	6,310,399 77	$153\tfrac{04}{100}$	$1\tfrac{4163}{10000}$	$0\tfrac{886}{1000}$	$0\tfrac{53.03}{100}$
1873	51,511,169 32	$59\tfrac{466}{1000}$	1,384,831,970	$229\tfrac{49}{100}$	19,608,555 07	11,867,197 63	7,741,357 44	$210\tfrac{42}{100}$	$1\tfrac{4159}{10000}$	$0\tfrac{857}{1000}$	$0\tfrac{55.89}{100}$

105

Comparative Statement, showing Cost of Road, Number of Passengers Carried, Earnings and Expenses, and Percentage of Increase and Decrease from 1864 to 1873, inclusive.

Year.	Cost of Road and Materials on hand.	Percentage of Increase or Decrease compared with year 1864.	Passengers One Mile.	Percentage of Increase or Decrease compared with year 1864.	Passenger Earnings.	Passenger Expenses.	Net Passenger Earnings.	Percentage of Increase or Decrease of Net Passenger Earnings compared with year 1864.	Earnings per Passenger per mile, excluding Mail and Express.	Expenses per Passenger per mile.	Net Earnings per Passenger per mile.
1864	$32,302,271 90	...	146,873,005	...	$4,268,910 30	$2,825,748 31	$1,443,161 99	...	Cts. 2 62/100	Cts. 1 92/100	Cts. 0 70/100
1865	33,271,889 04	3 2/1000	204,564,393	39 28/100	6,016,891 87	3,687,193 75	2,329,698 12	61 43/100	2 68/100	1 80/100	0 86/100
1866	30,392,257 71	5 913/1000	139,085,550	5 30/100	4,403,565 97	3,448,403 70	955,162 27	36 81/100	2 83/100	2 48/100	0 35/100
1867	30,189,965 97	6 539/1000	126,443,234	13 91/100	4,033,828 15	3,347,353 91	686,474 24	52 43/100	2 86/100	2 64/100	0 22/100
1868	31,171,362 51	3 501/1000	133,198,302	9 81/100	4,002,010 69	3,420,466 23	581,544 46	59 70/100	2 71/100	2 57/100	0 14/100
1869	34,292,295 20	6 161/1000	144,728,652	1 46/100	4,052,753 44	3,168,236 13	884,517 31	38 70/100	2 51/100	2 19/100	0 32/100
1870	35,595,146 19	10 20/1000	150,850,087	2 71/100	4,215,572 35	3,012,287 97	1,203,284 38	16 62/100	2 49/100	1 99/100	0 50/100
1871	36,404,780 03	12 700/1000	152,918,042	4 12/100	4,385,899 50	2,976,738 76	1,409,160 74	2 36/100	2 53/100	1 94/100	0 59/100
1872	44,740,893 35	38 538/1000	173,842,748	18 36/100	4,866,560 01	3,218,181 45	1,648,378 56	14 22/100	2 45/100	1 85/100	0 60/100
1873	51,511,169 32	59 466/1000	177,479,020	20 84/100	5,008,200 36	3,573,107 53	1,435,092 83	0 56/100	2 48/100	2 01/100	0 47/100

You will note that these tables include the years 1864 and 1865, during which large amounts of Government freight and a large number of troops were carried over your road. The results of the year 1866 more clearly give the normal condition of freight and travel. Yet we have had the calculations by comparison made with the year 1864, giving you ten years' working. These tables merit study, and we will not weary you with detail, except to call your attention to a comparison between the years 1864 and 1873, where you will note—

1. That with an increase of $59\frac{466}{1000}$ per cent. of capital, there was a gain in tons carried one mile of $229\frac{49}{100}$ per cent., and a gain in freight earnings of $210\frac{42}{100}$ per cent., while the rate of compensation received for carrying one ton one mile was reduced from $2\frac{48}{100}$ cents to $1\frac{4159}{10000}$ cents per ton per mile, and expenses from $1\frac{89}{100}$ cents to $0\frac{857}{1000}$, and the profit per ton only from $0\frac{59}{100}$ cents to $0\frac{5589}{10000}$ cents per ton per mile; thus showing that while the charge for moving freight was reduced $1\frac{641}{1000}$ cents per ton per mile, the expense of doing the work was reduced $1\frac{33}{1000}$ cents per ton per mile, and the profit was only brought down $\frac{311}{100000}$, or one-third of a mill per mile per ton.

2. The passenger travel will not, of course, show such favorable results, as the outlay on the road was mainly to carry freight; but it shows, as between 1864 and 1873, that with an addition to the capital of $59\frac{460}{1000}$ per cent., the passenger travel has increased $20\frac{84}{100}$ per cent., and the cost of carrying one passenger one mile from $1\frac{92}{100}$ to $2\frac{7}{100}$; while the net earnings have decreased from $0\frac{70}{100}$ to $0\frac{47}{100}$ cents per mile.

The increase of cost in carrying passengers is due to—

1. The increased number of trains.

2. Increased comfort in the cars.

3. Use of the Pullman cars.

4. High speed of trains.

The slow growth of the passenger travel in the last ten years, showing an increase of only two per cent. per year, and the increased cost of carrying a passenger a mile, suggests very forcibly the question whether your Directors, to meet the competition of other roads, are not furnishing the traveling public with facilities beyond the necessities of the case, and at too great a sacrifice of profit in making no difference in charges for transportation per mile between slow or fast trains, plain or elegant cars, medium-weight cars, or the heavy, track-destroying Pullman cars. Competition has run wild as to western travel; the accommodations which the traveler to Chicago, St. Louis, or Cincinnati receives on your fast lines, when considered in relation to the money he pays for them, shows the absurdity. To furnish on these fast lines a through car from each of these cities, without reference to the number of passengers, entails a constant loss to your treasury, as it does to that of other roads pursuing the same policy. Railroad companies will be driven by their absolute needs to adopt the juster principle of charging in proportion to services rendered. The lessened receipts of passengers per mile is due to the competition between trunk lines and the extended introduction of commutation tickets.

From this statement of the workings of increased capital put into your main line, it will be near enough to note that for every million of dollars invested since the year 1863 there has been an increased annual profit of $280,000, taking your profit in 1873 as a basis.

This gratifying result shows that all the addition to capital put in the main line has been well invested. Yet, as trade and travel increase, much more money will be required. The termini at New York, Amboy, Philadelphia, Pittsburg, and Baltimore, will continue to need enlargement, and with this increase of trade comes a demand for additional equipment, shops, machinery, track, and all the appurtenances necessary for the working of a railroad.

It seems to be a problem, to those unacquainted with the working of railways, to explain why additional traffic requires such continual outlay of money to move it. Yet we have shown the practical working and given the solution of the problem, in that after a road reaches a certain stage of development, as did your road in 1864, every dollar invested moves a much larger proportion of tonnage than the dollar originally invested could do, and thereby earns a larger percentage of profit.

So true is this, that the question of expense of increased facilities and the increasing trade is annually estimated by your officers, and provided for on the basis of the profit which this increase of investment of money will bring to your treasury. Their calculations will be interfered with at times by causes beyond their control,—such as in 1873, when they had been spending money freely in enlarging their facilities to meet the expected increase of traffic, and when the panic came, affecting their trade as it did that of the whole country; but, with the return of general prosperity, these expensive improvements will be found to be of great value and fully remunerative.

Probable Financial Demands of the Main Line.

How soon the trade of the country will recover from its present paralyzed condition we cannot tell; but no one doubts that it will recover and be again prosperous, and it is wise even now to look forward and make some calculations for the future.

There is another bountiful harvest in all parts of our country. This crop will have to be handled and moved in some manner, and it will bring some price. The very moving of a great crop gives employment to many machines and to many hands. The coming of better times must be hastened by the creation of values arising from an abundant harvest. Again, when prosperity comes to us, and every machine and every man is employed, it is hard to foresee how rapid the increase of their combined productions will be. But we have some data to depend upon—found in the workings of your road during the past ten years, from 1864 to 1873. By referring to the table, we find in the ten years the capital was increased $59\frac{400}{1000}$ per cent., or per year, nearly six per cent.; and that the tons of freight moved one mile increased $229\frac{49}{100}$ per cent., or per year, nearly twenty-three per cent.

Now, while the increase of capital is not in arithmetical but in geometrical progression, yet, if we take six per cent. on the capital on January 1st, 1874, viz., $51,511,169.32, being the amount invested in the main line, as a basis for the wants of the Pennsylvania Railroad for 1874, it will give about $3,000,000 as the amount required for enlargement for this year, which should give a proportionate increase of twenty-three per cent. on the tonnage moved one mile in 1873. It may not require so much for this year's actual business, and yet 1875 may demand a much more liberal outlay.

The expenditure of money for enlargement is not uniform over the length of the road, nor year by year. In some years the expenses will be very much greater than in others, on account of the character of the improvements. But we should not be surprised to find that the experience of the past ten years on your road would furnish a nearly reliable basis for the future, and we feel satisfied we are not far wrong when we estimate for your main line an additional outlay of three millions in 1874, and of near four millions in 1875.

As another evidence of the approximate accuracy of the above estimate, and of the truth of a former assertion as to the large proportionate increase of percentage of profit on every dollar invested, after a road reaches a certain status, which your road reached in 1864, we submit an interesting estimate to show further how much increase of traffic may be estimated before the limit of capacity is reached, the cost of the required improvements, and the profit that should be made—

1. There can be moved on the present main tracks of the Pennsylvania Railroad, between Pittsburg and New York, a traffic in passengers and freight seventy-five per cent. greater than that moved in 1873.

2. To move this increased traffic promptly and safely there will be required—

Forty miles of additional third track or middle sidings, costing $25,000 per mile,	$1,000,000 00
Three hundred locomotives, at $13,000 each,	3,900,000 00
Five thousand freight cars, at $650 each,	3,250,000 00
Two hundred passenger, baggage, and express cars, at $5000 each,	1,000,000 00
Increased siding room and other terminal facilities at Pittsburg, Altoona, Harrisburg, Philadelphia, and New York—say thirty miles of sidings, at $25,000 each,	750,000 00
Increased depot facilities and real estate at terminal points, say	3,000,000 00
Enlargement and extension of shops, engine-houses, &c., to take care of the additional motive power and rolling stock, say	1,500,000 00
Total,	$14,400,000 00

III

Let us examine and ascertain what these figures mean.

1. The main line, to be worked to its full present capacity, viz., seventy-five per cent. increase over business of 1873. By referring to the table, we find the traffic of 1873 to have been 1,384,831,970 tons moved one mile, or an average of 3,890,000 tons passing over the whole line from Pittsburg to Philadelphia, and 177,479,020 passengers carried one mile, or an average of 498,536 passengers carried over the same distance. Seventy-five per cent. increase on this would give an average through tonnage of 6,825,000 tons freight and of 872,438 passengers.

2. If the rates received for carrying freight and passengers and the cost of doing the work preserve the same proportion as in 1873, the net freight earnings would amount to $13,547,375 52
And the net passenger earnings to . . 2,511,412 44

    Total, ... $16,058,787 96
Add amount to receive from miscellaneous sources to be same as in 1873, . . . 269,253 47

And the total profit would be . . . $16,328,041 43
Total net earnings in 1873 were . . . 9,445,703 74

Or an increase of profit of $6,882,337 69

3. The capital invested in cost of main line and materials on hand January 1st, 1874, was $51,511,169 32
The additional capital required as above would be . . . $14,400,000
Add for additional material, say 4,600,000
                       19,000,000 00

Making capital and material cost . . . $70,511,169 32

That is, for an additional investment of capital of thirty-seven per cent. there would be an increased profit of seventy-three per cent.; or, every million of dollars invested would pay a profit of $362,228. We have shown you that for each $1,000,000 invested between 1873 and 1874 there was a profit of $280,000. The increased profit we now show you is a logical result of the fullest use of your road, and making the largest possible amount of money out of it.

To compensate for a possibly too low estimate of capital required to do this increased business, we have, on the other hand, the lower cost per ton for moving freight and passengers, arising from the less *pro rata* expense in every department of the road, which should make a very large item.

But these figures also include the line to New York, which, by the same character of calculation, would show an increased profit of $1,294,163 91
Profit in 1873, ... 1,725,551 88

Or a total profit of $3,019,715 79

Adding this to profit on the line from Pittsburg to Philadelphia would make a total yearly profit on each $1,000,000 invested of $430,342.

If the same *pro rata* rate of increase of freight and passengers should continue in the future as in the past ten years, viz., twenty-three per cent., it would take but little over three years to reach the figures named, which would require an average of $6,333,333 per year; or, if it is reached in five years, an average of $3,800,000. So that our estimate of the future financial needs of the main line must be nearly correct.

After these figures are reached and the line is worked to its utmost capacity, very heavy expenditures must be made to prepare additional through tracks to carry the traffic, which will for a time reduce the *pro rata* profit made on additional investments.

ARTICLE V.

Capital Account and Earnings of all the Railways under the Control of the Pennsylvania Railroad Company, tabulated in Systems.

We here present a condensed statement of the length, capital, receipts, expenses, and net earnings of the above systems or groups of railroads, including the Delaware and Raritan and the Susquehanna Canals.

Systems.	Total Miles.	Capital.	Receipts.	Expenses.	Net Earnings.
*Northern, or Fort Wayne,	1,707.6	$87,597,336 57	$19,351,020 26	$11,982,704 17	$7,368,316 09
†Southern, or Pittsburg, Cincinnati and St. Louis,	1,318.0	85,859,720 52	11,369,036 83	10,184,282 43	1,184,754 40
Baltimore and Potomac,	92.0	9,915,505 97	381,536 73	381,466 80	69 93
‡Eastern, or Pennsylvania,	2,816.0	214,895,112 16	51,933,320 18	35,010,161 54	16,923,158 64
	5,933.6	$398,267,675 22	$83,034,914 00	$57,558,614 94	$25,476,299 06

* The figures include returns of Indianapolis and St. Louis and Cleveland Railroads.
† The figures include returns of Vandalia Railroad.
‡ The figures include returns of Pennsylvania Canal, four hundred and eight miles long.

Systems.	Average Cost per Mile.	Average Receipts per Mile.	Net Expenses per Mile.	Net Earnings per Mile.
Northern, or Fort Wayne,	$51,316 54	$11,332 28	$7,011 42	$4,320 86
Southern, or Pittsburg, Cincinnati and St. Louis,	65,040 00	8,625 99	7,727 07	898 92
Eastern, or Pennsylvania,	76,312 18	18,442 00	12,432 00	6,000 96

The Fort Wayne system has nineteen hundred and sixty-six miles of single track.
The Southern system has fifteen hundred and four miles of single track.
The Pennsylvania system has thirty-one hundred and fifty-nine miles of single track, of which about six hundred miles are double track, and a large proportion laid with steel rails.

A study of these tables will be interesting and instructive. We will note some of the more striking points.

The tables show—

First.—The effect on profits caused by cost of construction, which is due to the topographical character of the country traversed, to the economy with which the road is built, and to the character of payment, whether by cash, insuring fair prices, or with stock and bonds, as certainly causing high prices to be paid.

Second.—The effect on profits caused by the ability of the country through which the road passes to furnish freight and travel in sufficient quantity and number of passengers at paying rates.

These tables show why the Pennsylvania Railroad system, with its long line of branches and its four hundred and sixty-nine miles of canals, pays so well. The capital this system stands charged with, including as it does the equipment, is represented at a moderate cost, while the local trade and travel on most of its various lines is abundant and profitable to transport. The Fort Wayne group of railroads represents a higher cost than they should. Yet, in comparison even with present prices of work and material, they could not be replaced at the same figures; and their results show the profitable effects of a large local trade and travel, which more than make up any loss from the through trade to the East and *vice versa*, and leaves a fair balance of profit to the owners and lessor.

The tables also reveal the true causes of the poor results of the Southern, or Pittsburg, Cincinnati and St. Louis system, which are—

1. The extravagant cost of the lines. With the exception of the line east of Steubenville, the roads pass over a very favorable country for building railroads.

2. From the inability of a country, chiefly agricultural, through which most of the lines pass, to furnish sufficient travel and traffic and at prices to make the roads profitable.

3. The drawback of the last point is so great as to affect the advantages that might be expected from a connection with the cities of Cincinnati, Louisville, Indianapolis, Chicago, and St. Louis.

4. It also teaches that the minimum of expenses at which lines of railroad can be run is much higher than is generally supposed.

The whole number of miles of railroad in the
United States in 1873 was 70,651
Whole number controlled by the Pennsylvania
Railroad Company, ... 5,933.6
Or of the whole number of miles the Pennsylvania Railroad controls $8\frac{398}{1000}$ per cent.
The total capital of all the railroads in
the United States is given at . . $3,784,543,034 00
Of which the Pennsylvania Railroad
controls 398,267,675 22
Or $10\frac{52}{100}$ per cent.

Yet, taking these different systems as a whole, comprising 5933.6 miles of lines and representing a cost of $398,267,675.22, their net earnings amount to $25,476,299.06, or an average of 6.39 per cent. on their cost. To appreciate this result, you must fully understand what it means. It embodies the workings and results on the 5933.6 miles controlled by you, and shows that notwithstanding some lines were imprudently built, and others built during the war at very high prices, and all the errors that may have been made, yet, under a scale of prices unprecedentedly low, and at rates which, if foreseen, would have prevented the building of many of these lines, the average profit has been as high as 6.39 per cent., or more than one-half the dividends which the Pennsylvania and some other companies are able to pay their stockholders.

The result of the above calculations shows that all the roads controlled by the Pennsylvania Railroad Company in 1873 earned $6\frac{39}{100}$ per cent. on their entire capital and bonded debt; that the roads east of Pittsburg earned $7\frac{87}{100}$ per cent., and the Pennsylvania Railroad proper, after paying interest and losses on her leased lines, earned for its stockholders $12\frac{22}{100}$ per cent.

ARTICLE VI.

Use of your Road by the Cars of Private Persons or Companies.

In the early history of the American railway, the companies arranged to furnish the power and the transporters the cars. After a time this was changed,—the companies furnishing both power and cars; and, still later, as the business of the companies increased, the policy was again changed so as to encourage large transporters to furnish their own cars. This has been the adopted policy of your Company for some years, the transporter paying the tariff rates on the freight and being allowed for the use of his cars over any part of your road and for any kind of traffic. Under this policy a number of companies use your road with satisfactory results to both parties. To the railroad company it saves investment of capital, and avoids the difficulties and jealousies that always arise in brisk times in the distribution of cars, while it practically requires fewer cars to carry the same amount of tonnage,—for the private transporter will get better service out of his cars than the railroad company can do, and this because such cars are proportioned in number to the wants of the transporter, are built for one character of freight, and run between fixed points. To the transporter it pays a fair interest on the investment of capital and secures a larger tonnage for the road, because the cars are kept in more constant use, and the shipments are not delayed for want of cars.

In the case of the Union (now owned by the Pennsylvania Company) and the Empire Transportation Companies, the same general policy is carried out, and differs from the other transportation lines on your road in two respects—first, they use many different railroads, the length of your road being but a small proportion of the entire length of roads used; and, second, they are allowed compensation or derive profits from the use of their cars, in addition to the ordinary wheel toll and car service, to an amount sufficient to cover the expenses of warehouses, soliciting and shipping agents, scattered along and at the termini of the roads they use.

The use of your road for the transportation of cars owned by private persons or by companies, though under the same general policy, has not been objected to, while the same use by the Union and Empire Lines has met with general disapproval. If the principle is good in the one case, we do not see why it is not good in the other. The argument that the railroad company should have all the possible profits is as applicable to one as to the other. Yet just here lies the question. Any one conversant with the working of the transportation department on your road must acknowledge the wisdom of allowing the market cars, the line cars from the Cumberland Valley and other roads, the coal, lumber, ore, and pig-iron cars of companies, to use your road; while with the other lines the objection against them is one more of suspicion than of knowledge or principle,—of suspicion, lest the Pennsylvania Railroad Company is not receiving from these lines a fair price for the facilities afforded, and lest they take away business from your cars for which you have provided stations and agents; in other words, whether they do not use the facilities provided for your own business to their advantage without paying a sufficient compensation therefor, they selecting the highest-paying freight, and leaving your road to carry the lowest classes.

The legal right of any individuals or corporations to use the road of this Company as common carriers is protected by the charter and repeated decisions of the courts.

We do not feel competent to determine the question of the sufficiency of the rates received by your Company for the use of your road and its facilities, but are satisfied of their general correctness, from the prices charged, or car service allowed local companies on other roads, and from an examination of the contracts of the last of the "Through Freight Lines,"—"*The Empire Transportation Company*," with several other companies in the same latitude, such as the Philadelphia and Reading, the Lehigh Valley, and the Central of New Jersey. The terms of these contracts are not precisely similar, yet in their working there is no practical difference. The contract between your Company and the Empire Company is based upon the true principle—that of your Company participating in the profits from increased rates for freight, the charges against the Empire Company being reduced to a fixed percentage of the moneys received from the freight carried.

1. The Empire Transportation Company.

We here enter on the consideration of a subject that has attracted very general attention, and with very great differences of opinion,—the relations of the above-named company with the Philadelphia and Erie Railroad and with your Company as lessees.

Let us carefully study the conditions of the case that a correct judgment may be formed. The primary object of your Company was to attract and build up a profitable traffic on the line of the Philadelphia and Erie Railroad. The question at once presented itself, how was this to be accomplished? As the possible trade was two-fold, one local and the other foreign, coming from other roads, two methods were open—

first, for your Company to furnish the cars for the local trade, and for the foreign trade to make arrangements with connecting roads for interchange of business and forming of through lines; or, second, to make such arrangements with a private company as would draw and secure foreign trade to the Philadelphia and Erie Railroad. As to business originating on the line of the road there was, of course, no trouble; but in attempting to draw traffic from the West, this difficulty was met with—the railroads over which foreign traffic could come were confined to the Atlantic and Great Western at Corry and the Lake Shore at Erie, which roads are in the interest of either the New York and Erie or the New York Central Railroads. This fact clearly disposed of any possible contract with either of those roads to form a line for through freight either to or from Philadelphia or New York, by way of the Philadelphia and Erie Railroad. The negative position of those roads to the interests of the Philadelphia and Erie Railroad developed another fact, that while no through co-operative line could be formed, all the traffic that could be drawn to the New York lines was solicited and obtained by transportation companies who used not only the main lines of the Lake Shore and Atlantic and Great Western roads, but held contracts with most of the other railways, especially in the North-west, and thereby drew the trade to those lines. It was evident then that the only opening left to obtain traffic for the Philadelphia and Erie Railroad from the West was to establish similar agencies.

Experience in the West has demonstrated that a railway cannot determine the route or destination of traffic originating on its line, and certainly has no controlling influence on trade at competitive points. Elements independent of the way of carriage first determine the destination of freight. After that, questions of time, safety, rates, &c., fix the route. With so many competitive points in the West, the railway companies recognize their true interests in furnishing every facility to the shipper of freight, and do not attempt by possible hindrances or unwise charges to defeat his interests, resulting, as it would, to the injury of the railway companies.

So intermixed among the western roads is the passage of freight that railway companies cannot make arrangements among themselves to work it successfully, and there is an absolute necessity for the intermediate presence of a third party, whose relations to all the companies give them access to their different roads. A company organized purely by the railway companies to do this kind of trade has been tried, and has not proved successful. It lacks the force, energy, interest, and immediate responsibility which a private company, working for its own interests, furnishes.

The transportation companies are, therefore, a necessary product of the peculiar character of western traffic, and are indispensable to every well-managed trunk line between the East and the West to fully meet the wants of the public.

With a full knowledge of the complication of this business and the work that must be done to draw trade from the West and North-west from the New York lines, and carry it over those lines to Erie or Corry and there pass it to the Philadelphia and Erie, the last question, then, for the Pennsylvania Railroad Company to decide was, whether they should enter upon this peculiar kind of railroad business or make arrangements with a transportation company to perform the work. The practical difficulties in the way of its being done by the Pennsylvania Railroad Company, and the amount of capital and extended connections required, will be best shown by giving some data of the Empire Transportation Company.

This company owns four thousand five hundred cars of all

kinds; has contracts with five thousand three hundred and ten miles of railway to furnish cars, &c.,—of these three thousand five hundred and ninety miles lie west of Erie; uses in its business sixteen thousand six hundred and forty additional miles of railway. It also owns eighteen large steam and sail vessels on the lakes, plying between Erie and western ports; at Erie it has two large elevators and expensive docks; in the city of New York it has to provide accommodations for receiving and distributing freight. To transact this large business a large number of agents must be scattered over the twenty thousand miles of western railways. With this condensed sketch of its operations, you will bear in mind that all the freight the line obtains in the West is secured by competition with other lines, and requires live, active agents at all points, and that the success of this company depends on the closest attention to its interests at every point.

To your committee it is evident that, first, the Pennsylvania Railroad Company had not $8,000,000 of capital to spare to put into this branch of business; second, that by the lease the Pennsylvania Railroad Company is not required to go off the Philadelphia and Erie line to solicit trade, and that it could not manage the peculiar character of this competitive traffic with success. It is one of those cases where a public corporation would fail in managing as closely and economically as a private corporation. In the one case the agents would be salaried officers; in the other, by salary and an interest in the stock of the private corporation much greater efficiency is secured.

The fact of the New York and Erie, the New York Central, and other large railway companies having made such arrangements with private corporations, is certainly some evidence of its propriety. And more than this, though the Pennsylvania Company has absorbed the Union Line, and it does not now exist as an active company, yet the experience of that company—which is the exponent of the experience of your executive officers—causes them to continue the practical organization and preserve the name of the Union Company. There is in the very nature of the case so much less red tape or form to be gone through with in making contracts, adjusting losses or damages, &c., with companies like the Union Transportation Company, that a shipper will always prefer sending merchandise by such companies, though at somewhat higher charges, rather than by the cars of the railroad company. This is a practical fact and cannot be overcome. So much for the western business.

The next important question in connection with the working of this line is in the transportation of oil from the Allegheny region. This region is the centre of very active competition among the leading railroads to the east, from the enormous tonnage it affords, and to secure it very great expense has to be encountered and very considerable risk.

To those of the stockholders unacquainted with the peculiarities of this trade, we give a few items of the kind of work that has to be done by the transporters, and illustrate it by the Empire Transportation Company. They have laid about four hundred miles of iron pipe, traversing the whole oil country, to connect the wells with the tanks built by them at the different stations on the railways. They are at a large outlay for pumps and appliances, have to build peculiar cars for carrying the oil, which are worthless for other purposes and are at a much greater risk of heavy loss from fire, and operate a complete private telegraph line through the oil region. To watch and take care of all this property requires a large, skilled, and expensive organization. It is a kind of work which a private corporation can do, but which one like the Pennsylvania Railroad Company cannot do as well.

This company also acts as transporter on the line of the Philadelphia and Erie Railroad, and in some instances on your main line. In these respects, it occupies precisely the same position as other parties using your road with their cars.

To give you a better conception of the amount of freight furnished by the Empire Company and carried over the Philadelphia and Erie Railroad to points west of Erie, and from points west of Erie to the east, we add the following for the year 1873:—

Tons of freight carried east,	318,352
Tons of freight carried west,	95,724
Total,	414,076

We also add the number of tons received from and sent west by the lake line owned by this company—

Tons of freight sent east,	161,355
Tons of freight sent west,	24,086
Total,	185,441

By the contract with the Pennsylvania Railroad Company the Empire Line is prohibited from carrying live stock, being confined to merchandise and oil. The result of this is, that no live stock is carried over the Philadelphia and Erie Railroad, while the Lake Shore Railway carried east through Erie, in 1873, three hundred and ninety-six thousand tons of live stock; and it shows the impossibility of taking freight away from the Lake Shore Line at Erie.

The same result will be shown by reference to the passenger travel. Your Company, finding that the through passengers will not leave the Lake Shore and Atlantic and Great Western roads, have wisely adapted the passenger trains on the Philadelphia and Erie Railroad to suit and develop the local travel, thus, by decreasing speed, saving heavy expense.

In addition to the competitive tonnage given above, (five hundred and ninety-nine thousand five hundred and seventeen tons,) the Empire Transportation Company moved an oil tonnage over the Western Pennsylvania, Allegheny Valley, and Pennsylvania Railroads to the seaboard of three hundred and fifty-three thousand three hundred and twenty tons, making the total competitive freight given to the Pennsylvania Railroad Company, on its different lines east of Erie and Pittsburg, nine hundred and fifty-two thousand seven hundred and thirty-seven tons.

Again, your Company makes use of the Empire Company's organization to solicit freight, and thereby successfully meet the competition of rival lines for traffic at local points on your main line and branches, such as Lancaster, Harrisburg, Carlisle, and Chambersburg. This character of work, while unprofitable to the Empire Company, saves to the Pennsylvania Railroad Company the expense of a corps of soliciting agents.

2. *The Pullman Palace Car Company.*

This company supplies your roads east of Pittsburg with about one hundred sleeping and drawing-room cars, worth, on an average, $15,000 for each car, or, for all, $1,500,000; and the roads west of Pittsburg with seventy cars, worth $1,050,000.

They furnish a valuable and indispensable accommodation to passengers, for which they are paid by the traveler, and are an entering wedge to the true principle of charging in proportion to services rendered.

There can be no question as to the entire ability of your Company to do this work as well as it is done by the Pullman Car Company. In the matter of investment there could not be much difference. You now have invested in this company—

$770,000 eight per cent. bonds, (with power to change, in three years, into an equal amount of stock at par,) worth $770,000
1233 shares stock, at par, paying twelve per cent. dividend, ... 123,300
$893,300

It would require an additional investment of $616,700 to fit your lines east of Pittsburg with the necessary equipment.

As to profit. Their cars, transported over your lines, make a profit quite equal to those on any other equal number of miles; and if they can make a dividend of twelve per cent., counting in their unprofitable lines, the same expenditure of money would probably bring you greater profit, besides having the absolute control of the cars and the agents.

On the other side, we recognize difficulties in the legal position of the Pullman Company under existing contracts—the question of your legal power to make an extra charge for such accommodation—whether the patents held by the Pullman Car Company are absolutely necessary to build an acceptable sleeping car, and other practical questions, and would therefore recommend their submission to the wisdom and discretion of the Directors.

But one point we desire very plainly to urge and insist

upon: that the public, who use the Pullman cars, should pay more to the railroad company than the small additional sum paid to the Pullman Company. They do not pay enough for the facilities and accommodations afforded.

We may sum up our conclusions after this long discussion and after acknowledging that they are almost entirely contrary to our impressions when we began the investigation, partaking as we did of the common prejudice against the introduction of such companies on your lines, as follows:—

1. The policy of encouraging private persons or corporations to avail themselves of their legal right to use your road is correct, and is conducive to the interests of both parties when a proper rate is charged.

2. That the work of the Empire Transportation Company is of that peculiar and special character that it cannot at this time be replaced by any organization your Company could form to do the work so promptly, so economically, and with such satisfaction to shippers and such ultimate profit to the Philadelphia and Erie Railroad Company and to the Pennsylvania Railroad Company.

3. The Pennsylvania Railroad Company works the Philadelphia and Erie Railroad at cost,—receiving no profit except for what trade and travel may pass over the line from Harrisburg to Philadelphia, or other lines in which they are interested,—and your Company is certainly under no obligation to enter upon a large outlay of capital, such as would be involved in replacing the investments of the Empire Transportation Company; and though largely interested in the stock and bonds of the Philadelphia and Erie Railroad Company, yet the Pennsylvania Railroad Company cannot be expected to furnish all the capital and take all

the risk to benefit the balance of the stockholders and bondholders. We have not heard of any proposition from the other stockholders to make up their share of such required capital, though constant efforts have been made to induce your Company to shoulder this burden.

4. The question of rates charged and allowed to private transporters and to the Empire Company we cannot undertake to discuss. We are willing to leave their decision to the Directors of your Company. The percentage of dividend paid by the Empire Transportation Company, viz., ten per cent., and the market value of its stock varying not much from par, would indicate that its profits are not unreasonable.

5. There is a tendency in such companies to verge too far in looking after their own interests, and there may be an inclination to infringe upon the interests of your Company. That this has been done is generally believed. It is, therefore, the more necessary that the officials and employees of your road shall be entirely free from any interest in such lines, and that the attention of the Directors be especially directed to the details of the working of these companies.

ARTICLE VII.

Coal Lands.

The coal properties owned wholly or partly by your Company in the anthracite regions of our State are located in the Lykens Valley, at Shamokin, near Hazleton, and at Nanticoke Dam, in the Wyoming Valley, and embrace an aggregate of twenty-seven thousand nine hundred and fifty acres.

The Lykens Valley

Coal property is situated about twenty miles north-east from Millersburg, on the Susquehanna. The lands lie in a contiguous block, extending about nine miles, containing an area of nine thousand two hundred acres. No other company has access to these veins.

In addition to the nine thousand two hundred acres of coal land there are about three thousand acres of valley land, mostly valuable for agricultural purposes. Owing to the great depth of the basin at Bear Gap, as well as the quality of the coal contained therein, this coal land is of more value than any equal number of acres in the State.

The quality of the Lykens Valley coal, which thus far has been the only coal worked in this region, is well known. The price averages at least seventy-five cents per ton higher than any other anthracite coal, with an increasing popularity and a demand resulting therefrom which makes this, perhaps, the most valuable coal property in this country, not only from its vast extent, but from the fact that its coal, from its quality, is at all times in active demand. A very low estimate from actual surveys makes the workable coal of these lands equal to one hundred million tons.

The precise ownership of your Company in the Lykens Valley coal lands is somewhat difficult of exact expression. The Summit Branch Railroad Company virtually owns the whole region, because in addition to its own property it owns seven thousand three hundred and nineteen out of a total of nine thousand eight hundred and eighty-three shares of Lykens Valley Coal Company's stock. It has also claims for money advanced to the latter company amounting to $964,889.38. This is equal to the full ownership of the Lykens Valley property. Your Company owns forty-three thousand eight hundred and four shares out of eighty-two thousand five hundred shares of the whole capital stock of the Summit Branch Railroad Company. You acquired the ownership of this stock at different times and different prices, the aggregate cost for the whole interest being $1,495,024.64.

There are four collieries and breakers upon this property, with an average daily capacity of three thousand five hundred and fifty tons.

The purchase of the Lykens Valley property, under the circumstances, was most judicious. It was purchased at an early period, at very low figures, and entirely in accordance with the most conservative policy. The Northern Central Railway, a majority of whose stock is held by you, was dependent upon these regions for traffic to Baltimore and intermediate points. Securing these coal properties gives this road and your road, east from Harrisburg, and the canal interest you hold from Millersburg, a valuable tonnage for a great many years to come.

The value of this coal property must increase; and in the

judgment of the committee the management is wise in its determination that its product shall be mined only as the trade may demand, at largely remunerative prices. It is a property so valuable, so accessible to the market, with a coal that must increase in popularity and in consumption each year. The property should be worked, therefore, only to supply the immediate demand. Full rates are charged to transport this coal, so that your Company obtains, in addition to the profit on the coal, a very large sum for its carriage. The manifest skill, care, and vigor with which the business is conducted is deserving of special commendation.

The Summit Branch Company, in addition to the above, owns property, not immediately located in this valley, worth perhaps $150,000.

Shamokin Region.

The ownership of the Shamokin coal field is in the Northern Central Railway Company (as lessee of the Shamokin Valley and Pottsville Railroad) and in your Company, but the property is worked by the Mineral Railroad and Mining Company. Its stock amounts to fifty thousand shares, at twenty dollars per share, of which one-third is held by the Pennsylvania Railroad Company and two-thirds by the Northern Central Railway Company. This company's coals are of good quality, but inferior to those mined in the Lykens Valley region.

The true policy of the company is that no more coal shall be mined from this property than will supply the southern and western demands, except what may be required for the Boston market, which, as a rule, pays a satisfactory profit.

The collieries have been held by the company but a few years, and during that time heavy improvement expenses and bitter competition along all the lines of transportation controlled by your Company have prevented much progress or profit, except in the way of feeding the retail trade at Boston.

There are eight collieries upon this property, with an average aggregate daily capacity of two thousand four hundred and seventy-five tons.

The land embraced in the Shamokin region amounts to seven thousand eight hundred and eight acres, all underlaid with coal with veins in shallow basins. The principal veins thus far worked are from eight to ten feet thick, and lie in close proximity. The portion of this property held by your Company cost $1,092,574, and has, perhaps, a cash value to-day of $1,300,000.

The Hazleton Property,

Owned by your Company exclusively, consists of from two thousand one hundred to two thousand two hundred acres, and is yet undeveloped, except by a small expenditure for explorations. These explorations would seem to establish the fact that this property is underlaid almost entirely with coal. The larger part of this property (say one thousand seven hundred acres) was bought at a cost of $180,000. Afterwards the Nicholas Rope tract was purchased. It contains about four hundred and forty acres, and cost in Pennsylvania Canal bonds, at par, $99,000, with an expenditure of some $14,000 or $15,000 for explorations, taxes, and interest, making the whole Hazleton property stand about $295,000.

From the situation of the property, and from the results of borings, shaftings, and testings of various kinds by competent and skillful men, it would appear as if this property, bought very low in comparison with its real value, will prove to be one of the most valuable coal properties of the

State. From the notes of the geologist, as well as from the borings made under the direction of Major Anthony, these gentlemen have no doubt but the Mammoth vein underlies a large portion of the property. If this be the case, this property, which cost an average of $180 an acre, including interest on the bonds and expenses of explorations, is clearly worth from $1000 to $1500 an acre. At $1000 an acre, which is the lowest sum named, it would be worth $2,200,000.

From this coal property there is a direct route over the Danville, Hazleton and Wilkesbarre Railroad to the Northern Central and Philadelphia and Erie roads, as well as to all lines controlled by the Lehigh Valley and Lehigh Navigation Company.

The Susquehanna Coal Property.

This company was organized in 1869, and the property is owned jointly by your Company and the Pennsylvania Canal Company, the whole being under the control of the former. The original purpose of the investment was to produce increased tonnage for the canal, and at the same time, particularly during the winter months, to provide your rail lines lying west of this point—the Northern Central, &c.—with tonnage which otherwise would be diverted to other channels. The area of coal land embraced in these properties is five thousand eight hundred and twenty-three acres. It lies on both sides of the Susquehanna, at Nanticoke Dam. The cost, including discount on bonds partly used as purchase-money, was about $555 an acre—making $3,232,067.48. Adding improvements, buildings, &c., it amounted on the thirty-first day of last December, to $3,931,323.57,—of this amount your Company has paid $1,555,109.77. The Susquehanna Coal Company has authority to issue six per cent.

forty years bonds, with coupons, amounting to $2,000,000, of which amount $1,283,000 have been issued, with the principal and interest guaranteed by the Pennsylvania Railroad Company. The stock consists of fifteen thousand shares, at a par value of $100 per share, amounting to $1,500,000, of which the Pennsylvania Canal Company owns $500,000 and your Company $1,000,000.

The larger portion of the land at Nanticoke lies on the south side of the river. The breakers are erected in very favorable locations, so that shipping facilities can be had by canal and railroad over the Nanticoke and Lehigh Valley and Lehigh and Susquehanna Railroads, to the market at South Amboy. The bridge at Nanticoke is now completed, and increased rail connections with our lines, via the Lackawanna and Bloomsburg Railroad to Northumberland, will largely increase the tonnage, enabling all the collieries to work fully up to the demands of the market. They are now greatly in want of winter transportation southward.

It is believed that the charge for transporting freight for other roads across the bridge will more than pay the interest on the investment, besides giving enlarged facilities to our own interests and saving about twenty-five cents per ton on all the coal from the south side shipped east, west, and south.

Perhaps no property in the State is better located for the mining and shipping of coal than the Nanticoke property. The product all naturally centres in the bay or basin, where coal can run to the breakers and be shipped over the canal of the Susquehanna Valley to tide-water, or by rail, as before referred to.

There are four breakers completed, with an aggregate daily capacity of twenty-eight hundred tons,

The improvements now in course of construction upon this property are of the most thorough and substantial character, and when completed, which will be in the next three or four years, will make its capacity nearly one million tons per annum. The improvements going on now consist of two shafts—one double, the other single—and a slope with breaker, from which shipments can be at once made.

The propriety of expending a large sum of money, so as to increase the immediate product of these mines, seems very doubtful. The property should be worked so as to give what tonnage may be needed, in connection with coal purchased, to fill the contract made with the Lackawanna and Bloomsburg road, amounting to two hundred and fifty thousand tons per annum, *when it cannot be purchased elsewhere*, and to supply the canal with what may be carried over it profitably. The danger is that a desire to give tonnage to the canal and to the railroad will deplete the property, without receiving therefrom an equivalent for the valuable product shipped. We are glad to have the assurance of the President of the coal company that the future policy in the Wyoming region shall be as above suggested.

The management of the Nanticoke property, on the whole, is vigorous and efficient. No one can visit the anthracite coal fields without being struck with the rapidity with which these lands are being depleted of their rich deposits. The belief is entertained by some of the best informed and most practical men that twenty-five, or even twenty years, of such mining and shipping as is going on at present will make the anthracite fields of Pennsylvania so difficult and expensive to operate as to bring into market the almost as yet untouched bituminous coals in the western part of the State, which are practically inexhaustible. An increased price per ton, not much beyond the present price, will enable the bituminous coal fields to ship their mighty product to all the eastern markets. Already the shipments of this coal to the seaboard and to Buffalo and other points north are attracting notice, and the increase of tonnage within a brief period is very remarkable.

Our main line and branches in the western portion of this State run through more than two hundred miles of country which abounds with this great source of wealth. The tonnage from it must increase each year upon our road, and become ultimately a source of immense revenue to the Company. Indeed, no man can at present estimate the future production and shipment of bituminous coal east, for use in our own and perhaps in other countries.

Policy of Railroad Companies Owning and Working Coal Lands.

It has become the custom in these latter times for great railroad companies to take into their own hands interests that, in the early history of the country, were supposed to belong exclusively to other corporations or individuals. This policy is not only of doubtful propriety, as affecting the interests of the people of the Commonwealth and the country, but involves financial problems that may confuse and confound the wisest of managers. The Philadelphia and Reading Railroad Company is an exemplification of this modern idea. Twenty years' experience alone can solve the problem undertaken. Embarrassments of a serious character arose as to a uniform supply of coal from private parties, with the difficulty of controlling labor; but it is a gigantic undertaking for any corporation to attempt, unless under the most favorable circumstances, to prepare and control the production it carries. Your Company, of all the railroads in the State, is farthest removed from the necessity for any such policy. It is purely a company for transporting supplies shipped over the main road and its branches. Its locality must make it increase in value as the country increases in wealth and the West increases in population, because each new acre tilled, and each new town built, must send over this great artery of commerce a share of its productions, and receive in return the necessities and comforts of life. You can, therefore, only afford to enter into the purchase and control of coal properties, in any section of the State, to conserve some local interest entered into. If this view be sound, the managers of your Company would seem to have been debarred from having anything to do with coal properties in the anthracite region except for special use along the line of the road, or in the Lykens Valley or Shamokin regions to give tonnage over the Northern Central Railway and the canals connected therewith. The judgment of the committee is that the purchase, joint ownership, or control of coal properties by your Company should have begun and ended with the Lykens Valley and Shamokin properties. The purchase of the Hazleton property was in pursuance of the policy of acquiring large interests in the anthracite coal fields, which the late administration thought they were forced to adopt, which purchase, as well as that at Nanticoke, is believed to have been injudicious.

Your committee have every reason to believe that the present management of the Company will shape its policy into wiser and more conservative channels. If purchases and undertakings have been injudiciously entered into, they should not be timidly or hastily abandoned, but so directed as to recover, if possible, what may have been endangered. This ground has been taken by the present management, and it is hoped will be rigidly adhered to.

It is believed that in the future all the energy and genius of the management will be devoted to conserving and developing the interests already possessed.

Transportation.

As the subject of transportation has occupied considerable attention, it may be well to suggest that what seems to be absolutely required in the movement of coal, from both the Lykens Valley and Shamokin regions, is that the Company should be placed in position to control eastern shipments which now largely depend upon the Reading Railroad. The purchase of six hundred or one thousand cars by the Summit Branch Railroad Company would enable shipments to be made directly to Greenwich, on the Delaware, instead of over the Reading Railroad to Port Richmond. When there is a brisk demand for cars the Reading Company may use their cars for mines of their own, and thus limit the production of these properties. This ought to be changed, and the Summit Branch Company or your Company and the Northern Central should furnish cars for the full movement of coal produced when the profit is satisfactory. The freight from the Lykens Valley region last year was four hundred and fifty-nine thousand one hundred and fifty-nine tons, and from the Shamokin region two hundred and forty-seven thousand three hundred and seventy-six tons. The average cost of carrying this coal last winter was as follows:— To Dauphin forty-two and one-half cents, to Richmond one dollar and eighty and thirteen one-hundredths cents, making a total of two dollars and twenty-two and sixty-three one-hundredths cents. If this was carried to Greenwich over your line, retaining the forty-two and one-half cents charged on the Northern Central Railway, it would have a haul of one hundred and twenty-five miles, and a rate per ton per mile of one and forty-four one-hundredths cents; or, if prorated with the Northern Central, the rate for both companies would be one and fifty-four one-hundredths cents per ton per mile. The net profit on this business (now given to competing lines) would amount, from the Lykens Valley trade alone, to $200,000 per year. The amount paid for freight to the Reading Company on coal from the Lykens Valley, during 1873, was $406,208.30. The total amount of freight paid to the Reading Railroad Company for the transportation of coal from the Lykens Valley and Shamokin regions, during the year 1873, was $521,933.84.

The shipment of the Susquehanna Coal Company's product east over the Lehigh Valley and Susquehanna Railroads, instead of west and south over the Northern Central and other lines owned or controlled by the Company, has occasioned some criticism. It is but proper to give the facts in the case. *First.*—No coal is shipped east over the lines named, except such as our western and southern market will not profitably take. *Second.*—The amount shipped east is only about one-third of the whole product. In giving direction to shipments, the officers of the coal company have to regard the profit on the coal as well as the interests of your transportation lines.

In shipping west and south, you carry the coal to its destination over your own lines, except sixty-four miles over the Lackawanna and Bloomsburg Railroad. In shipping east, your own lines do all the work, except from Warrior run to Philipsburg, a distance of ninety-six miles. It would therefore be to your advantage for shipments to be made exclusively to the West and South, so far as transportation is concerned. But at times one size or variety of coal is dull of sale in one market and active in another. Hence it is most profitable to ship coal to the market that will pay the best price for it, even if it goes a greater distance over some other road.

Annexed is a summary exhibiting the acreage, cost, and estimated value of the coal properties:—

	No. of Acres.	Cost to Penna. R. R. Co.	Present Estimated Value.
Lykens Valley coal region,	12,200	$1,495,024 64	$7,000,000
Shamokin coal region,	7,808	1,092,574 00	1,300,000
Hazleton coal property,	2,119	295,000 00	2,000,000
Wyoming Valley coal property,	5,823	1,555,109 77	2,236,884
Totals,	27,950	$4,437,708 41	$12,536,884

The above we believe to be a correct estimate of value, but the properties being recently purchased and only partly developed, we have taken them at cost in estimating the Company's assets.

ARTICLE VIII.

Finances.

1. Mode of Control of Other Roads.

We desire here to say a few words on the policy we think should be adopted towards the branch and connecting railways.

1. Where it is possible, and the interests of both parties can be justly taken care of, we think you should absorb all the smaller companies into your corporation, thereby saving the annual expense of keeping up a separate organization, and securing thereby greater economy of management and simplicity in the accounts.

2. Where it is not advisable to absorb, we think your policy should be to lease, and leases may be of three general kinds—

(1.) By paying a fixed rental.

(2.) By charging a fixed *pro rata* rate of receipts.

(3.) By working the roads, charging the absolute cost thereof, and receiving compensation for the use of engines, machinery, &c.

Where a lease is based on a fixed and fair present rental, which presupposes always that the business of the company will warrant it, the advantages to the lessee are—

1. That such a lease will grow in value to the lessee as the business or the trade on the road increases, and the railroad company, as lessee, may expect in time to receive increased profit.

2. The second plan is one of doubtful propriety. It unsettles the values of both parties, and while it may approve itself as a general principle, yet we think experience has shown it is an undesirable method.

3. The plan of working leased roads at cost has been thoroughly tried by your Company, and is peculiarly well adapted to the leasing of roads of uncertain value and of short branches, but is inferior in profit and advantage to your Company to the mode of leasing under a fixed rental, where the prospective growth and development of a road is clear and undoubted.

4. A strong motive for holding branch roads by lease rather than by ownership of stock or bonds is, that the continual decrease in the purchasing power of the standard of value will gradually lessen the value of bonds held as an investment. A dollar, to-day, will purchase either of material or labor but little more than thirty-three cents would buy fifty years ago. Then one dollar was the ordinary wages for a day's skilled labor—now from three to four dollars is demanded for the same quality, and the time shortened from twelve to ten hours. The discovery of gold in California and Australia, and the pouring into circulation of the vast sums produced in the mines of those countries, have been sufficient to effect this change, irrespective of the issue of paper money in the United States; and consequently, in a long term of years, the appreciation in the nominal value of a railroad bond, even though bought below par, will be apparent rather than real. On the other hand, the rental of a leased road, from the same cause, becomes every year less and less burdensome, the traffic and travel producing larger sums for their conduct, and the amount of rent exhibiting no corresponding increase.

We may here remark that this same cause will have its influence in making the leases and guarantees of the Pennsylvania Railroad Company and the Pennsylvania Company less burdensome and more profitable year by year. Though these may be just at present a drain upon the finances of the parent corporation, yet the irresistible progress of events and the logic of circumstances will, in the end, prove the value of those arrangements. The gradual filling up of the territory will provide travelers and freight, while the decrease in the value of gold will give more dollars in payment for services rendered by the roads—the rentals and guaranteed interest on bonds remaining stationary.

5. Again, by your absorbing and holding railways as lessees, instead of controlling them by owning a majority of stock, it releases and relieves you from adding largely to your capital, that you may be able to carry the stocks and bonds necessary to keep control of such railway. This point will be more specifically referred to hereafter.

2. The Necessity for the Pennsylvania Railroad Company's Managing the Finances of Roads under its Control.

We here, at the outset, meet with a difficulty. It would seem most proper that the large companies under your control as lessees or by majority of stock should take care of their own finances and furnish from their own property sufficient security to provide for any needed enlargement. It seems very objectionable that the money interests of all these companies should fall back on your treasury for the assistance they require, and on your credit to give them a standing in the market.

Yet we are convinced that it is out of the question to separate the financial management of these different companies from your own. The very fact of your taking an interest in a railroad company, while it helps the credit of that company, certainly causes the capitalist to expect the addition of your endorsement, and we are rather surprised than otherwise to notice how successfully your Directors have avoided this tendency. Yet the fact remains, and must be accepted, that the general control of the financial wants of all the railways in which you are interested must be in your hands and subject to your guidance.

To get, then, some conception of what this amounts to, we refer you to the statement showing the amount of stock, bonds, receipts, and expenses of these roads in 1873.

In addition to furnishing the capital needed for conducting the general business of these roads without floating debts, which, including the Allegheny Valley Railroad, amount to about $18,000,000, it will be necessary to provide for the payment or renewal of most of the bonds as they become due—that is, $180,000,000 bonds, within thirty years. This is of itself a great undertaking; and yet more, as the business of these roads increases an amount of money must be annually raised to pay for enlargements and extensions to meet the demand. With a small additional increase—say two per cent. on the $150,000,000 of capital—you would need at least $3,000,000 to be raised in some way each year, or even more than that amount, if the trade on the roads grows more rapidly than estimated.

You will agree with us that the taking care of these three items will add to the responsibility of your Directors, and we make the suggestions in this report, under the head of *Organization*, imperative.

Three somewhat compensating advantages accompany this responsibility—

1. You will control more completely the financial management of each road in which you are interested as endorser, guarantor, lessee, or stockholder.

2. By a wise comprehension of the wants of all your lines, you can the better regulate the whole question of extension and betterments over these lines, making the payments for the same less burdensome and more readily handled.

3. The concentration of the management of these finances in one board will simplify your intercourse with capitalists, who will the more readily learn to appreciate your securities at their true value, and not depreciate them by reason of their large amount. This is a school which our own capitalists need. It is sometimes difficult to make them understand that large operations can be successful.

3. Floating Debt.

It has been a characteristic of the management of your Company to prepare, in advance, to meet the wants and demands of the growing trade upon your road and its tributaries; and this has, at times, caused your Directors to raise money on their notes before realizing the necessary funds from its revenues or sales of bonds or stock. It is easy to see how any disappointment in the sale of such securities, or disturbance in the money market, would find them with a large floating debt, as in the fall of 1873.

A floating debt of a railway company is always an evidence of imprudent financiering; it throws a suspicion on the credit of a strong company, which is, of itself, a hindrance to the negotiation of its bonds, and is injurious in two ways—in subjecting the company to paying high rates of interest, and in lowering the percentage at which the capitalist will purchase their bonds.

To the credit of a weak company it is disastrous, for it is the confession of its standing before investors of money; and the rates of interest such a company must pay will, in the end, prove ruinous to it.

These principles are applicable to your Company. A temporary injury was done to its credit by the existence of a large floating debt.

It is, then, evident that the first duty of your Directors is to provide for the payment of all its floating debt.

The shareholders should express their will and judgment, first, that no future floating debt shall be made except—as must arise in all kinds of business—for purely temporary use; and, second, that it is safer and more to their interest to delay improvements until the funds are provided to pay for the same, as hereinbefore suggested.

4. Construction Account.

We strongly recommend to your Directors the continuance of the policy of the Company to charge to *expenses* a fair proportion of what would otherwise be placed to *construction*. The advantage of this policy is seen in the comparison we have shown of the real cost of your road with that which is represented in the *general account*.

It gives so much additional security to your stock and bonds, requires so much less money to pay dividends, and renders you the better able to successfully compete with other roads. Again, it is but fair to do so, for there is an annual integer of destruction and depreciation in values that have been charged to construction account, and which can only be made good by replacing it by other work and charging that to expense account.

5. Reduction of Capital Stock and Funded Debt.

At the risk of repeating ourselves, we think it better to aggregate what we have said in previous portions of this report, *on the reduction of capital*, in a separate article. No one will question that the true policy of your Company is to keep the amount of capital stock and bonds at as low a figure as possible consistent with your true interests. We have heretofore suggested the two ways in which this can be done—

1. By leasing or absorbing such roads as come in their terms within the range of safety to your treasury, and when such roads are leased, to dispose of the stock and bonds you may hold of that company.

2. By sale of all securities that will bring an approximately fair price, and which can be parted with without injury to the Company.

By the previous policy of the Company there has been brought into your treasury a very large amount of stocks and bonds of companies which have been leased by you or by the Pennsylvania Company, and the proceeds of these purchases have been used to improve such roads. These stocks and bonds, in the great majority of cases, were bought at low figures. But the policy of your Directors has been, first, to take hold of some roads in poor condition; second, to keep the stocks and bonds in your treasury until they should increase in value and pay you a large profit; and, third, to enable you to purchase and hold large amounts of stocks and bonds of leased roads, it has been necessary to issue a large amount of your own stock and bonds, thereby increasing the sum required for your semi-annual dividends and the interest on your bonded debt. This has been a policy full of danger to your interests. It led your Directors, in times when money was abundant and seeking investment, to enter upon operations which otherwise they would not have approved. It is no new thing to see a company *destroyed* by the burden of *non-productive investments*, which, *if kept strictly within proper bounds*, would have been grandly successful. This is a recognized danger to all large corporations or associations of private capital. It was this policy which led your Directors to the recommendation and issue of the consolidated mortgage.

For a striking illustration of these points, we need go no further than the action of your board during the past few years. If the true policy of leasing other roads and of selling their securities as rapidly as they accumulated had been adopted, though at some sacrifice to your treasury at the time, you would have disposed of, before the year 1873, at least $35,000,000 of securities, all of which would have brought fair prices, thus entirely obviating any necessity for the large increase in the year 1873 of your stock, amounting to $14,873,538, and of bonds to the amount of $8,073,476, —in all $22,947,014. This policy would have provided a sufficient surplus to have avoided a floating debt.

The fruits of this experience should be shown in your determination that hereafter constant efforts shall be made to keep your capital stock and bonded indebtedness at the lowest figures consistent with the true interests of the Company.

6. *Funded Debt.*

We have, in the last article, referred to the true cause of the issue of the "Consolidated Mortgage." In addition to furnishing means for increasing the operations of the Company, it affords a channel to refund the bonds already issued as they become due. This mortgage is so peculiar in its construction, that we think it may be well to give its leading characteristics.

1. The main object was to furnish a mortgage that would be sufficiently comprehensive to provide for the issuing of successive series of bonds limited to a fixed total sum, without requiring the creation of a new mortgage as each series of bonds would become due. It is, therefore, made a continuous lien to secure the payment of bonds, to be issued from time to time, as the Company may determine, to the extent of $100,000,000. The series of bonds to be issued may vary in amount in the rate of interest not to exceed seven per cent., and in time of payment, and when one series becomes due and is paid, or for any other reason canceled, the Company may authorize the issue of an equal amount of bonds, to become due at some other fixed time; the only restraint being as to rate of interest, and that the amount of bonds outstanding at any one time shall not exceed $100,000,000; but by the law of the State, the amount of bonds issued can never exceed the amount of capital stock paid in, therefore, before the whole amount of bonds provided for ($100,000,000) can be issued, $100,000,000 of capital stock must be paid in.

2. There are included in this mortgage, as additional security, various bonds and stocks held and owned by the Company, to the value of $50,000,000, all of which bonds and stocks are perpetually and forever pledged, and without regard to the amount of bonds at any time outstanding, except under certain conditions, viz.:—

(*1.*) That the securities themselves may be replaced by others of equal value.

(*2.*) That the proceeds of the securities may be used to purchase, for cancellation, bonds issued under this mortgage.

(*3.*) That the proceeds of the securities may be released to the value of improvements made on any part of the Pennsylvania Railroad, from Philadelphia to Pittsburg, of the leased roads of the United Companies of New Jersey, the Delaware and Raritan Canal, on the leased premises of the Philadelphia and Erie Railroad, or in the purchase by the Pennsylvania Railroad Company of other property, real or personal.

3. There has been issued and sold under this mortgage one series of bonds to the amount of £2,000,000 sterling, at six per cent., to become due in the year 1905. A second series of bonds to the amount of £3,000,000 sterling has been authorized at six per cent., to become due in the year 1915, part of which last series is sold, and arrangements made for the balance. This sale is to cover the payment of second mortgage bonds to the amount of $4,865,840, coming due April 1st, 1875, about $2,700,000 dividend scrip outstanding, and the balance to be used in paying the floating debt and for other purposes.

If so large an amount of bonds had not been issued, or arranged to be issued, under this mortgage, we should have strongly and decidedly recommended the withdrawal of the bonds already issued, the annulling of the mortgage, that the securities therein placed might be taken out and used to meet the wants of the Company, on the ground that they were not necessary to give ample security to any bonds that might be issued under the mortgage.

This will be readily seen by the recital of a few facts. As this mortgage provides for the issuing of bonds to the amount of $100,000,000, it was right that equivalent securities should be provided as the bonds were issued. We therefore start with a capital stock security of $68,744,495, representing an outlay and valuation of $94,398,483 on the main line alone, which no one will question affords ample security for an issue of bonds equivalent to the amount of capital stock now issued. This would have furnished the basis for an issue of bonds to the extent of $38,749,875 in addition to the $29,394,600 heretofore issued, and left a margin on the main line alone of $21,253,608, besides the additional security that would be derived by the investment of the proceeds of those bonds. This, with the bonds, stocks, and other property now owned by the Company, would give to the bondholders as security $217,121,653.17 in actual values to secure $68,744,495. In other words, when your present bonded debt shall have reached $68,744,495, there will be as security property to the value of $217,121,653.17; and to show the ample security provided for the whole amount of the mortgage, should it ever be required, we have the main line from Philadelphia to Pittsburg, representing a value of $94,398,483, on which the net earnings in 1873 were $9,445,703.74, less taxes and rent of Harrisburg, Portsmouth, Mount Joy and Lancaster Railroad, being nearly three millions of dollars more than sufficient reserve to pay the interest on the entire amount of $100,000,000 that may be ultimately issued under the mortgage. This, without allowing anything whatever for the investment or increased value of the property to the amount of about $101,000,000, to be derived from bonds and stock required to make the issue of $100,000,000 of bonds possible. When we add to this the certainty of largely increased revenues from this greatly increased property, it shows most plainly to the bondholder that his security is more than ample.

We therefore reiterate our opinion, (1.) that these securities were not needed to give ample security for any bonds that might be issued under that mortgage. (2.) That it was a waste of credit for which the interests of the Company have suffered—for the presence of those securities in that instrument has not rendered the bonds more marketable nor added to the price received. (3.) That the holding of securities for a rise while borrowing money from stock and bond holders at high rates to carry them was unwise. (4.) That the placing of available securities in a mortgage was of itself an anomalous act. (5.) That the placing of those securities in this mortgage was contrary to the true policy of the Company in keeping down its capital to the lowest amount. (6.) That, in fine, the mortgage itself was not, with proper views of finance, a necessity, for at the time of its execution more money could have been realized from the sale of those securities than from the bonds issued under and secured by the mortgage.

We might name other weighty reasons, but the above are certainly sufficient to characterize the act of placing those securities in this mortgage as imprudent and improvident financiering.

To show you its practical working, we need go back only to the fall of 1873.

This mortgage was executed on July 1st, 1873, and the available securities and assets of the Company were thus put out of their control. When the panic came in September, the Directors found their available assets tied up, and they could not pay cash for current wants. An earned dividend was paid in scrip at fifteen months, and the credit of the Company was seriously affected, and in its tenderest spot, namely, in the confidence of its stockholders. We need not quote the prices at which the stock was sold, nor remind you how the earnings and the savings of many years were lost to many people,—and all this injury and suffering was the result of this incomprehensible and unbusinesslike act of tying up available securities while at least there was any possible chance of their being needed. With these securities in the possession of your treasury during the panic, very little financial skill would have paid your floating debt as it became due, cashed your bills for supplies, paid your dividend in cash, saved you credit, and very many people heavy losses which they could not well bear. We deem this full statement necessary in order that the stockholders and capitalists may know why the Pennsylvania Railroad Company was placed in the fall of 1873 in such an unfavorable position.

The position in which this locking up of your most available assets placed the finances of your Company plainly leaves but one course for your Directors to follow, and which we most strongly recommend:—

(*a.*) To apply rigidly the provisions of that mortgage as to releases of securities to provide for payment of betterments, &c. made on the different railroads, as therein provided.

(*b.*) By consolidating with or leasing railroads now in your interest upon favorable terms or at a fair rental, which will relieve you of the necessity of continuing to own these stocks and bonds now necessary to retain the control of such roads.

On the resuscitation of credit a large proportion of these securities can be sold at a fair price, and the proceeds applied, first, to pay for all improvements, betterments, &c.; and, second, to the reduction of the funded debt of the Company by the purchase of its bonds.

5. *Future Profits of the Company.*

We have discussed, at several places in this report, different points affecting the future of your Company, and would here summarize, by more formally stating that we see nothing in its present condition, taking everything into consideration, which will unfavorably affect its future success. On the one hand we have shown that there will, in all probability, be no claim on you as guarantor on the Western lines, and on the Eastern lines your absolute annual loss, under all the conditions of your liability, will not exceed $280,000, with the possibility of some ultimate loss from the amounts charged against different railroad companies for advances to pay interest on bonds, loss in working, &c., now considered as good.

While on the other side you are justified in expecting improvement in the workings of all the lines you control. These roads have been put in good order, at great expense, from which should result a large *pro rata* profit on the same amount of business, with ground to count on a much larger trade, bringing with it increased profit. With these two favorable elements, this class of roads will, year by year, lessen your liability as guarantor.

As to your road proper, the advantages arising from the very great expenditure of money in the different departments of the road—the motive power and the cars—the increase of shops and tools, depots, terminal facilities, &c.—the decrease of wages and cost of material used—will all tell very favorably on the cost of transportation; while the tonnage carried (temporarily affected in 1874) will show hereafter a constant increase.

A stop being put to investments in foreign corporations, your finances will speedily assume a better and healthier condition, for the demand on the treasury can now be measured.

The finances of the companies you control will improve for the same reasons, and their stocks and bonds will appreciate in value. Summing up these items, and looking at the past business and net earnings of your Company, we feel quite safe in recording our opinion that the net receipts of the Pennsylvania Railroad Company will, after the present exceptional year, be equal to fifteen per cent. on a capital stock of $70,000,000, which will give you a reliable dividend of ten per cent. and leave $3,500,000 for developing the general interests of the Company.

An interesting statement of the net earnings of your main line and branches, and of the Western railroads for the first six months of 1874, has been already referred to in Appendixes B and C.

6. Summary of the Present and Future Financial Wants of the Pennsylvania Railroad Company and of the Railroad Companies it Controls.

Gathering our estimates from the different parts of this report, we present them in a condensed form.

1. For the Pennsylvania Railroad Company.

There is needed, to pay off your floating debt, consisting of bills payable, acceptances, and dividend scrip, about	$7,311,000
There will be annually, for twelve years, an amount to pay the State of Pennsylvania, on account of purchase of Philadelphia and Columbia Railroad,	460,000
There will be a necessity to provide for the payment or renewal of the mortgage bonds as they become due, viz.:—	
In 1875, for the second mortgage, amounting to	4,865,000
In 1880, for the first mortgage, amounting to	4,970,000
In 1910, for the general mortgage, amounting to	19,558,760
In 1905, for the consolidated mortgage, amounting to (£2,000,000 @ $4.85 = $9,700,000)	8,245,000
And to furnish means to meet the cost of improvements and enlargements consequent on increased trade about, per year,	3,500,000

2. For the Railroads controlled by you.

To relieve them of their floating debt, not including the Pennsylvania Company, and including the Allegheny Valley Railroad Company, ... $18,000,000

To pay and replace with other mortgages bonds coming due, in different amounts, between 1873 and 1919, the whole amounting to . 180,000,000

To furnish means to make improvements and enlargements for increased trade, per year, 3,000,000

These statements comprise the financial outlook into the future, and we recommend they should be provided for as follows:—

(1.) *For the Pennsylvania Railroad Company.*

The floating debt should be paid, as already recommended, by sale of securities now held by your treasury, and by securities released on account of betterments, &c., as provided for in the consolidated mortgage. Being incurred on account of them, they should furnish the means wherewith this debt should be paid. The annual payments to the State should be met, as they always have been, by the profits, and charged to expense account, and, after paying the shareholders an annual ten per cent. dividend, the remainder should be used for betterments. If there is any deficiency, it should be made up by sale of securities, as above. The bonded debt of your road can be readily paid and replaced.

(2.) *For the roads controlled by your Company.*

The Floating Debt.—This amount is scattered over so many roads that, while it adds up to large figures, yet is not heavy, except in the case of the Allegheny Valley Railroad, which is now being arranged to be funded for twenty years, before which time it is believed that the Company will be able to take care of it.

The funded debt of these companies is large. That you may thoroughly understand the future demands from this cause, we give in Appendix E a very full statement of the amount of bonds, the year they become due, and the company by whom issued. A careful examination of this list will satisfy you that there is nothing in this part of the financial present or future that need cause any anxiety.

The money needed to extend the facilities of the roads to meet increase of traffic can, in many instances, be furnished by the surplus profits of the individual road, and in others the betterments may form a good security for an increase of stock or bonds. A resurvey of the whole concentrates the financial difficulties in one item—*the floating debt of the Pennsylvania Railroad Company and of the companies controlled by her.* Let these be arranged for and put out of the way, and there will be an end to any financial trouble connected with your Company,—the expansion so prevalent in past years being ended, your Directors should hereafter manage the interests of your great corporation cautiously and prudently, developing the local business on all your lines, and placing that of the other connecting lines on a steady and firm basis, uninfluenced by personal or road rivalry.

ARTICLE IX.

IN REGARD TO THE ELECTION OF DIRECTORS BY DIRECTORS, AND THE ACCEPTANCE OF LAWS WITHOUT THE SANCTION OF THE STOCKHOLDERS.

In our examination of the different laws passed by the Legislature of the State of Pennsylvania affecting your Company, we find several which have authorized the Board of Directors to accept the same, and thereby made them binding on the Company and part of its organic law. Among them is a general law authorizing boards of directors to elect from among the stockholders additional directors, who shall be vice-presidents and receive pay for their services.

We do not think it necessary to make an argument against the propriety of acts of the legislature affecting the property and rights of stockholders being made subject to the approval of boards of directors. It is self-evident that all such laws should be submitted to and be approved by the stockholders, and we therefore have inserted a provision on the subject which will be found in our article on *Organization.*

We also disapprove of any legislation which empowers directors to elect other directors. It is equally clear that all such agents should be chosen by the shareholders, and be responsible to them, and we have also made a provision embracing this feature in the article above referred to.

ARTICLE X.

THE SOURCES OF THE EXISTING DISTRUST IN THE VALUE OF RAILWAY STOCKS AND SECURITIES.

There exists in the public mind a want of confidence in railway stocks as a means of permanent investment. It is feared by some that all moneys invested in railway stocks will ultimately be sunk and lost from the operation of the causes we will notice. This state of hesitation and doubt should not exist. There is no reason for it in the character of the investment. Well-located and well-managed railways will pay good dividends on the amount in cash invested in them. The causes of this want of confidence must then exist outside the nature of the case. Let us examine and find out, if possible, what they are; and we suggest, as the

First.—The meagre and incomplete reports of the directors of railroads made to the stockholders. Railway directors, in their reports, seem guided by the old adage—"that the least said is soonest mended." There is a tendency to limit their reports to the general results of a year's work, giving financial results and the economic workings, while the stockholders are left in great ignorance of the value of their own property. There should be in every report the fullest detail of these items, enabling each stockholder, at the end of a year, to make his own estimate of the value of his stock. But these reports should go further and give the most ample information as to the position of the road in its relations with other roads, and state fully all the facts that might influence its policy, its plans for the future, or its finances.

Second.—The tendency in the leading officials and managers of railroad companies to act as if the property they manage was their own. This is natural. Strong men, with their natural self-reliance, and from their more intimate knowledge of the particular interests of a company, are apt to assume the infallibility of their own judgment, and therefore grow impatient, and come at last to look upon a stockholder who may ask a question, or presume to criticise their conduct or plans, as an impertinent intermeddler, and the annual problem is how to get through with the stockholders' meeting without debate; showing, at least, a lack of confidence in the shareholders. These persons must learn to submit to the unwillingness of the shareholders to abandon their right of judgment, though that judgment should be wrong. They also overlook the weightier and more important fact that, apart from the right which shareholders have to discuss all matters affecting their interest, the directors and officials by this means lose the profit and moral support which shareholders, educated by a full discussion of the reports of the directors, would give them. We shall refer to this subject again.

Third.—The fear that the property of the company may be used by officials and favored employees for their own personal benefit. This has been done in several ways—by furnishing materials, such as coal, wood, lumber, and iron to the road; by being interested in companies using the road, in contracts for work, &c. It is not a question now with your committee whether these charges made against so many roads are true or not as to your road; but they are united in judgment in recommending to the stockholders to take such action as will prevent any official or employee in your service being interested in furnishing any supplies to your road, in any contracts, or in any company doing business over your road, its branches, or roads acquired by lease or otherwise. The law passed by the last legislature to carry out the intent of the new Constitution, to protect shareholders on this point, does not reach the evil. Before the stockholders can have proper confidence in the management of their property, they must know that the Directors practice on the maxim that purity of management can only be obtained when the Directors, officials, and employees are free from any complications which may affect the interest of your road, and that such rules are established and carried into practice as will prevent such persons from in any way using the road or the Company for their own profit. Any other policy than this is dangerous to the parties themselves, and certainly prejudicial to the interests of the shareholders.

Fourth.—In the case of the Pennsylvania Railroad Company, there has been an unsatisfied doubt in the minds of its stockholders as to the policy of private companies using the road. We have examined this question in a former article very fully, and have given our conclusions. Yet we are aware of the strength of the public prejudice and the almost insuperable difficulty in convincing the stockholders that such companies do not make more than their share of gains, and that they perform any service which the Company or companies could not do as well, and thus the shareholders receive more profit.

Fifth.—The tendency among railway stockholders to transfer the decision of all important questions to the board of directors.

In discussing the organization of railway companies, we

shall enter very fully into an examination of the proper relations between the shareholders and the directors. The existing relation, in almost every large railway organization, will show that the shareholders are almost a nullity as to their influence in the policy or management of their own property,—their main utility being in furnishing an audience to hear a report and voting for directors a ticket carefully prepared for them. The evils of this are apparent, and it is time for the shareholders to resume, or, more properly, assume, the direction and control of their property.

It seems very strange and unbusinesslike that the stockholders of the Pennsylvania Railroad Company have allowed the Directors such control of their property that they could lease railways, guarantee payments, and incur liabilities and accept laws, and all this without consultation and without the approval or knowledge of the stockholders. That the Company has not been financially wrecked is due more to the prudence of the Directors than to the wisdom of the shareholders.

Sixth.—In the constant tendency to extension and expansion, as shown in our railway history.

Herein lies, probably, the main cause of the doubt that hangs over railway stocks and securities and affects public confidence in them. No one acquainted with the business of our country would say there should be no such extension; and yet how far such extension should go is a very difficult question in most cases to determine, but more especially when it affects our leading railway companies connecting by their lines the East and the West.

The rivalry between these great lines has produced questions of extension in themselves difficult to decide, and there have been, and are likely to be, as human nature goes, questions of extension where rivalry comes in as a strong element to determine the matter.

There is also a fear that combinations of influential individuals are made for speculative purposes, to get rid of a poor investment, at a high price, by tacking it on to a successful railway.

There is also a temptation to encourage and assume liabilities for the building of extensions far in advance of the wants of the country, and these liabilities become a burden upon the guaranteeing corporation. In fact, while there is any country beyond the termini of the road or its branches, there is an almost irresistible temptation to go still further and follow population and production beyond their limits. The investing world recognizing this tendency —this fact—as a power in the management of our leading railways, rightly deems it dangerous to the security of bonds and value of stock, and thus, as heretofore written, a general want of confidence exists as to the value of the stock and securities of our leading railways; while, with prudent and proper management, these roads should offer the best means of investment of capital, and then all the moneys needed for proper extension would be promptly furnished.

The systems of roads controlled by your Company have been quite thoroughly canvassed in this report. They surely, with the tributaries beyond the centres they reach, cover enough ground to furnish the largest amount of business over your road, and the development of the lines embraced in these systems is fully as much as any one corporation can attend to, and your committee therefore most urgently recommend that such measures should be adopted by the stockholders as shall limit the board from extending their interests beyond their present bounds. And even thus limited, the committee, aware how, in times of great prosperity, a board of directors may be tempted to contract liabilities for extension within these limits, deem it wise and prudent that you should further require your consent to be given before any new guarantees or leases shall be entered into or liabilities incurred.

If your committee are correct in their views as to the causes of distrust as to the value of your own stock and bonds, as well as those of other companies, they think the passage of the resolutions covering the views herein set forth, appended to this report, will favorably influence the public mind by securing a reliable administration of the varied interests of this Company.

ARTICLE XI.

ORGANIZATION.

Your committee, impressed with the magnitude of the operations, connections, and liabilities of the Company, and with its certain future large extension of business, have felt it incumbent on them to consider the adaptation of the present organization to manage such great interests, and submit the following suggestions:—

The original theory of railway organization in this country was a Board of Directors, a President charged with the finances, and a Superintendent in charge of the management of the railroad,—the Superintendent being the only one who was either a professional engineer or an expert in railway management.

Experience has modified this organization by making the President the executive officer of the company, expecting him to be thoroughly qualified, and holding him generally responsible for its entire management. The Board of Directors are usually chosen for their supposed sound judgment, business knowledge, and integrity, and are generally unacquainted with the professional part of railway management. Being absorbed in their own private affairs, they cannot give the time, even if they had the knowledge, to do much more than stand before the stockholders responsible only for the honesty of the management,—to protect them from the improper use of the funds or property of the company,—so that the boards are almost wholly influenced in their action by the views of the President, and the power of the corporation quietly and surely glides into his hands. With this power, the President makes and unmakes Directors, thereby seriously affecting the *morale* of the board. It is natural, and in some respects right, that a President should have those in the board who will be influenced by and not be antagonistic to him. Yet the stockholders expect an independence in judgment and action which is not possible while the Directors are virtually appointees of the President. The facts thus briefly stated show two things—

First.—The working of the present form of most organizations weakens and destroys the influence and power of the Directors, rendering them of little use to the stockholders; and this is especially true in railway boards, where the Directors usually lack the professional knowledge that would make them useful.

Second.—It the more completely places the power and fortune of the corporation in the hands of one man—the President.

This is a fair picture of the general working of railway organizations in the United States. The same result is to be noticed in almost all our institutions, whether commercial, financial, or benevolent. It is a result of our enterprise, energy, and confidence. How often this is abused the courts of bankruptcy, the almost daily *exposé* of defalcations, the multitudes robbed of their rights, the destitution of the helpless and confiding, the sufferings of widows and orphans, victims of error, neglect, or crime in those to whose care they have confided their property, reveal a sad history.

It is true that the centralization of power in the hands of one competent man contributes largely to efficient working.

It secures (up to the point of his ability) prompt decision and a harmonious policy, as it is impressed with the thought of one mind. It saves from the effects of divided counsels, jealousies of officials, &c. A plan with such results may work well in a small corporation; but when applied to large corporations like the Pennsylvania Railroad Company (and many others in this country) it becomes a more difficult matter.

Take your own Company, now controlling nearly six thousand miles of railway and canal, involving a capital of nearly $400,000,000, and which, of necessity, will largely increase with the growth in population and productiveness of the contributing country, and two questions will force themselves on your consideration—

I. Is it wise, prudent, or just, that the almost absolute control of such vast interests should be placed under the power of any one man to designate its policy, control its working, determine its growth, and regulate its finances? Yet such is the practical fact under your present organization. Your corporation has grown to its present status under the inspiration and guidance of one master-mind,—of a man of honest intentions and remarkable ability. The experience of the past is our best guide for the future, and errors may be made profitable by being used for wholesome warnings. Are you willing to continue such a policy? Changes must take place in time, and under an incompetent, dishonest, or speculative President—which is by no means impossible—what havoc and destruction of values might be made of your property, causing deep disgrace and wide-spread suffering!

II. The operations of your Company have now reached the point where your committee think it has passed the power of any one man to manage its interests with that personal oversight and care which they demand. The number of questions involving important interests that are ever pressing for decision are beyond any one man's mental or physical powers to endure for any length of time. And the fact that the road and properties now controlled by your Company are located in at least eleven States of this Union, and many of these the largest of the States, whose laws and powers, as they affect the several corporations, require the most devoted attention, as well that all due care shall be taken to develop the traffic on all the lines to the highest attainable point, so that the interests of the stockholders may be protected, and secure to the public the greatest facilities at the least cost, accumulates an amount of labor that no one man can properly perform.

Under the present organization the effect is that, to avoid injury to the interests of the Company by delay in decision, many important questions are practically determined by irresponsible subordinates, or by the action of Directors, who are quite unprepared to decide such questions, and the body corporate necessarily suffers injury and loss.

Some of the doings of your late President and Board of Directors are evidences of that want of careful investigation and oversight which arises from the defects of the present organization, because it is out of the question for one man to perform the labor of acquiring knowledge of all the facts, to carefully digest them, and to decide at once promptly and rightly.

Again, your corporation requires in its management many men of the highest and most varied talent. Their education requires long time—it becomes a source of wealth to the Company—and you cannot afford to place them in such positions and impose on them such an amount of duties as will exhaust them, mentally and physically, in a few years of service. You should utilize this knowledge by careful nursing, and not exhaust its possessor by a stimulating process.

If, then, we rightly appreciate the condition of things in the organization of your Company, it follows—

1. That the present form of organization makes practical ciphers of the Directors, and this from no deliberate intention, but from the very necessities of the case.

2. That it as inevitably throws the power and control of this great corporation, with its immense interests, chiefly in the hands of one man; which is unjust, unwise, and imprudent, and if, in addition to these points, it is true that—

3. The successful management of these great interests is beyond the ability of any one man: it does seem clear to your committee that the proper time has arrived when you should carefully consider this grave and important question.

Let us then determine the true basis of an organization that will be the best adapted to manage your interests and produce the best results in profit to yourselves, to the city of Philadelphia, the State of Pennsylvania, and the great extent of country reached by your lines. And the problem is how to place all needed restrictions on your agents without affecting their ability to produce the best possible results, with a proper reservation of the rights and obligations of ownership.

If we examine the principles upon which an organization should be formed, we find—

(*1.*) That the STOCKHOLDERS, under the charter of the Pennsylvania Railroad Company, are the owners of the corporate rights and property, and the original and only source of power and authority.

(*2.*) That for the more convenient management of their interests, they select a certain number of DIRECTORS and MANAGERS, who are their agents or servants, to take care of and develop their property, under the instructions of the stockholders, to be wholly executive in their duties, and to be altogether guided by the general policy laid down and approved from time to time by the stockholders.

(*3.*) That these executive functions may be most successfully used and developed, it is necessary to provide, in the construction of the board, such a variety of talent, experience, and character as will make their united judgment approach most nearly to a perfect judgment; and,

(*4.*) That for still further convenience, and to place the managers under the most direct responsibility to the shareholders, THEY are permitted to appoint the other OFFICERS AND EMPLOYEES required to attend to the detail of the operations of the roads.

If this is the true conception of the fundamental principles of an organization, it plainly requires, for its harmonious working, a plan which, while

(1.) It will keep the absolute control of the Company in the hands of the stockholders;

(2.) It will also provide for a board of managers so constituted as to combine the greatest amount of skilled knowledge with business experience, broad and enlightened views, and personal integrity; and,

(3.) It will give the individual officers and servants the strongest inducements and the greatest possible freedom in working out the problems and advancing the science of railway management; thereby securing the best results of the combined energies and skill of the employees. It must inspire an *esprit du corps* affecting every man, from the President to the ballast-breaker.

With these views of the true principles of an organization, let us now consider, *first*, what powers should be reserved by the stockholders.

i. Clearly all legislative powers involving the determination of the general policy of the Company, the assumption of obligations, whether in issuing bonds, leasing railroads, guarantees of rental of other roads, of the interest and principal of the bonds, or of the acts of other companies, or the incurring of any liability outside the ordinary expenses of conducting the operations of the Company, and the approval or acceptance of all acts or laws, general or special, affecting the Company.

ii. What powers should be delegated to the managers or Directors? Their duties being executive, such powers only are necessary as will enable them to perform those duties, which are embraced under the two general headings of the finances and the road. We need not elaborate these duties—the titles are sufficiently suggestive.

There is another collateral duty. Being placed in such intimate relations with the detailed workings of the road, and studying and watching its growth, development, and interests, they should be the first to detect its wants, and thus be prepared to advise the shareholders, thereby adding to their executive functions those of an advisory character.

Having thus settled the respective powers and duties of the principal (the stockholders) and the agents (the directors), let us now consider—

The practice and experience of the English railway stockholders.

While we may not learn much from English and continental experience in the organization or management of railways, we may learn much from the relations of the shareholders to their directors. If we are rightly informed, the custom of the most important railway corporations in England is to have semi-annual reports made of the operations of the roads to the stockholders at their meetings. These reports give full accounts of the condition of the companies, showing the receipts and expenses of the road in operation, and of all other disbursements of money, reporting the balance of profit, if such there be, with a recommendation of amount of dividend to be declared. They also make a statement of the wants of the company for the next ensuing half year, other than ordinary expenses, covering such questions as extensions, leases, extraordinary outlays (giving reasons therefor), estimated cost, and suggestions as to how the money may be raised to meet these outlays. These questions are all submitted to the stockholders for determination. They are freely discussed, and, if necessary, are decided by a stock vote. This is a condensed sketch of their way of doing, and your committee think it secures several advantages—

1. The owners decide all important questions affecting their property.

2. It saves the managing and other directors from censure for failures or imprudent legislation, as all legislation is the act of the owners.

3. It protects from the charge of personal interest, which is so often made against railway officials in America.

4. It insures the provision of the means to pay for outlays before they are commenced.

5. It causes greater care in examination before the recommendations for new work are made. Extensions or leases are laid before the stockholders, which insures careful preliminary examinations, knowing they will be thoroughly

examined and freely discussed before being approved and sanctioned.

6. It has the good effect of educating the shareholders in railway matters, thus enabling them to form a proper judgment upon the recommendations of the board.

7. It has the effect of inducing capitalists to hold larger lines of a good stock, when they know they will have an important voice in the policy of the company, and in so far is a guarantee to weaker stockholders that their interests will be protected.

8. The result of this will be, that the stock will have a recognized and just value, will not be a mere foot-ball in the stock exchanges of the great monetary centres, and though perhaps paying less dividends, will have a higher and more permanent value than a stock subject to constant change.

Are not these results in perfect accord with the theory of organization we have presented? Will not the adoption of these principles tend to remove the distrust, doubt, and uncertainty that now prevail in regard to railway investments?

They may not be perfect, but are they not in advance of our system? A road may not progress so rapidly; it may lose something by slowness of motion; but will it not be safer and more profitable in the end? We think so, and we believe that a great step forward would be taken (while leaving the meetings annual, as they are now) by requiring full and complete statements as to the operations of the roads and of the wants for the year following, involving all questions of leases or guarantees, or any extraordinary expenses, to be determined by the shareholders; and to further require that, at or before the time of declaring a semi-annual dividend, the Directors shall publish the basis on which such dividend is declared.

Let us look more carefully into the proper constitution of the *personnel* of the Board of Directors. We have already intimated that the Board of Directors should be composed of men—some of them skilled in the science of railway management, others of business experience—of broad and enlightened views, and all of undoubted personal integrity. We have also discussed causes of distrust of railway securities existing among capitalists, and have shown you the tendencies of the present prevailing organization of railways to concentrate this whole power in the hands of the President; and, further, the alarming extent to which the assumption of the powers of the stockholders have been by legislative acts taken from them and placed in the hands of the servants of the companies— the directors. We have also demonstrated that the amount of labor thrown upon the President of the Pennsylvania Railroad Company by the working of its former organization was more than could be performed by any one man promptly and satisfactorily, and that the whole responsibility being on him, had led to this concentration of power by practically giving him the ultimate decision of all questions concerning the roads and affecting the policy of the Company. In this respect the new organization is an improvement.

The requisites, then, in the board, are to have, in addition to the President, (1) a sufficient number of men who are skilled in the different leading departments of the road and of finance, to aid him in his more immediate executive labors; and (2) a sufficient number of Directors who shall have had a business education, are generally conversant with finances, the value of property, the interests of trade, and a comprehensive knowledge of the productions and wants of the country, and who, in their personal character, are of the highest integrity.

To secure independent and responsible Directors, and to protect the shareholders against the dangers arising from one man, by virtue of his position as President, controlling the nominations for Directors, and thereby the officers and servants of every grade on the six thousand miles of road and canal under your control, we can recommend no better plan, which will be approximately effective, than—

1st. That at every annual meeting of the stockholders there should be a committee appointed, as was done at your last meeting, in accordance with a resolution passed by the stockholders February 1st, 1858, by which a committee of seven stockholders was appointed by the chairman of the meeting to recommend suitable persons for Directors, and to publish the names in a certain number of daily newspapers of the city of Philadelphia for a fixed time.

2d. That the stockholders may have time to examine the annual report, that it be published once, in at least three daily newspapers of the city of Philadelphia, at least two weeks before each annual meeting of the stockholders.

3d. That the skilled members of the board should be elected by the stockholders, and be held responsible to them for their acts in common with other Directors.

We submit a sketch of an organization of the board that seems to us would meet these requirements.

(*i.*) That of the number of Directors to be elected by the shareholders there shall be four—three of whom shall be professional railway men, and one of financial experience and ability.

(*ii.*) That of the three professional railway men, one shall be chosen as the President of the board, one may be charged more especially with the interests of your Company west of Pittsburg, and one may be charged more especially with the oversight and care of the roads which you own and control at and east of Erie and Pittsburg.

(*iii.*) These four members of the board shall form an executive council, of which the President shall be chairman. The council, of course, to be under the control of the Board of Directors as a whole.

(*iv.*) The President of the board and the three other Directors elected for especial service shall devote their time to the interests of the Company, and be liberally paid for their services.

This plan will not prevent giving the President ample powers for prompt executive action and for the successful performance of the duties of his office. We trust no man will ever fill this place who does not combine with a thorough knowledge of the road and the varied interests of the Company the highest executive ability, and the power, by his superior acquirements, of reasonably and justly influencing his co-Directors, and thereby producing harmonious action. The plan will not minify, but in fact magnify, the office. While it will protect the Company from the dangers of personal rule, it will also guard the occupant from a responsibility beyond what is proper and just. It will provide for a strong man being surrounded and aided by strong men, and throw a proper responsibility upon all the Directors charged with the interests of a Company on whose success the fortunes and happiness of so many people of all conditions depend.

We have gone thus far into the details of this plan of organization, not so much to determine those details, but rather to offer suggestions showing how smoothly and efficiently the plan may be worked. We have not touched upon many other questions, preferring to leave the details, in all respects, except as to Articles 1, 3, and 5, to the Board of Directors.

After having so carefully worked out this plan of an organization, we would now compare it with the present organization of your board, and ascertain the points of difference, and whether any practical difficulties exist that ought to prevent the adoption of our recommendations.

a. The present number elected by the stockholders is ten, by the city of Philadelphia three, and the Directors have the right to add to their number four skilled men to act as Vice-Presidents, making the number limited by the law seventeen.

b. We propose keeping the number of Directors to the number allowed by the charter, viz., thirteen. Four (including the President) to be skilled or professional men and nine non-professional.

c. There is no difference in the number of professional Directors in either plan. In both of these plans the professional Directors are to give their whole time to the Company, and they should be paid liberally for their services; the difference being that in the one case the stockholders elect their agents, and in the other the Directors elect them. We think we have established the principle that the stockholders should retain the power of electing their most important and responsible agents. If elected by the Directors they are responsible to the Directors, and are, in fact, the creatures of the President; while if elected by the stockholders, they are responsible to them, like the other Directors. Men of sufficient ability to occupy the position of Vice-President (or Managing Director, as it might be named) of the Pennsylvania Railroad will always be men who have been tried, and whose fitness for counsel as well as for action have been developed and demonstrated.

This plan, we believe, will secure to the Pennsylvania Railroad—

(1st.) The ability to manage all the varied interests of your Company.

(2d.) It will secure the independence of each member of the Board of Directors, and his individual responsibility to the stockholders.

(3d.) It will provide for the more perfect division of labor, and place responsibility where it properly belongs.

(4th.) It will secure by the executive council more thorough investigation of every subject, clearer comprehension and a better grasp of every point by the board as a whole, and insure prompt decision—the lack of which has been heretofore a serious, practical, and unavoidable defect.

(5th.) It will provide against many defects and dangers which we have heretofore pointed out in your present organization.

The plans we propose, affecting the powers and duties of the Board of Directors and their organization, are an innovation on the American system. The principle of paid Directors has, we believe, always existed in the management of English railways.

The general existence in American railways of the same difficulties that demand a change in the organization of your Company must be acknowledged, and if the companies are to be saved from ruin those difficulties must be met by all the great railway corporations of this country.

We append resolutions covering all the points of the organization we have discussed.

We have thus laid before you the plan of organization which we think best adapted for the management of the interests of your Company, and regret that we feel compelled to suggest any variation from it at this time. But to carry out this plan would require an act of the Legislature of the State of Pennsylvania authorizing you to elect Directors who may receive salaries; and by accepting such an act, your Company would at once be brought under and subject to the provisions of the seventeenth article of the new Constitution.

While we see nothing in this article that would necessarily produce any injury to your Company, yet, as there has been no judicial decision upon some important points, and as your officers apprehend difficulties which their experience in conducting transportation suggests, we would not hazard inflicting any possible injury on your Company, while the end we propose may be measurably reached, at least so far as establishing the principle that the stockholders shall determine who shall be their Directors.

We therefore propose that the committee who shall be appointed from year to year to nominate persons for Directors shall also, in consultation with the President, name the Vice-Presidents who shall be recommended to be elected by the Board of Directors, and that this plan shall continue until necessity shall either force your Company to apply for legislation, or the full meaning of the seventeenth article of the new Constitution shall have received judicial interpretation which shall not be unfavorable to your interests. When either of these conditions is met, then we earnestly recommend the adoption in full of the plan of organization we have reported. The system of organization which we have submitted for the assurance of your safety and the protection of your interests is altogether impersonal, having been written before the death of the late President, and is based on governmental principles immutable in their nature, sanctioned by the experience of ages, and equally important for yourselves and your servants.

While this investigation has been in progress, important changes in the organization and regulations of the business of the Company have been made. The death of the late President, who had been identified with the road since its inauguration, seemed to demand such action.

The present President appreciated the fact that with the changes made by time, death, &c., many modifications were needed to meet the existing condition of things, and on his acceptance of the office, called the attention of the Board of Directors to the subject, and urged that they should designate a committee to examine into the condition of the Company in all its departments, and all matters pertaining to its organization, and report such changes and regulations for the government of the service as in their judgment might be necessary.

This has been done, and they are now in force. We have examined them with care, and believe they cannot fail to be advantageous to the Company, inasmuch as they place additional restrictions upon power, concentrate duties, increase responsibilities, and place all the rules of the Company before each man connected with the service.

It will be perceived that rules and regulations made by the Directors may be changed by them; but by embracing these rules in the supreme law made by the stockholders, they are placed above the power of the Directors.

For the practical application of these views, we present for your consideration the resolutions annexed to this report.

ARTICLE XII.

RÉSUMÉ.

Your committee, before closing their report, by condensing its many pages into a few paragraphs, desire to give that which will be acceptable to most readers—the pith or point thereof.

(1.) We have given you a detailed explanation and introduced our valuations of the different items in the general account, as submitted by the Board of Directors, to December 31st, 1873, and have shown that the assets of the Company are worth $118,955,405.08 over and above its bonded and other indebtedness, and deducting the amount of capital stock issued to December 31st, 1873, leaves a surplus value of $50,810,930.08, making each share of stock represent $87.28, excluding any increased value in the anthracite coal interests held by your Company, and that each mile of single track represents a real value of $45,436, while on your books it shows but $19,728.59.

(2.) We have given you a detailed statement of your liabilities, as endorser of bonds of other companies, as guarantor of rentals for leases of railroads, both where you are the principal and where guarantor for the faithful performance of contracts by other companies. That as endorser of bonds you are liable for the principal and interest of $33,983,000—the annual interest of which amounts to

$2,106,440, and for the annual payment of $180,000—the interest of $3,000,000 of bonds, and a liability for rentals guaranteed of $13,862,319.94, on all of which there was a deficiency in 1873 of but $1,470,129.45, and this was confined to roads and interests east of Pittsburg. We have further shown you that, estimating for 1874, this amount will be largely reduced, and the actual loss from this cause should not exceed $280,000.

(3.) We have at great length discussed all the lines of railway in which you are directly interested, and frankly stated our opinions, with the reasons therefor, whether in censure or praise. For the western roads we have confidence that they will, with the increase of population and its diversified employment, gradually develop a profitable local trade, and that the surplus productions of the West will ultimately come to you in a more valuable shape, securing greater profit to your road in its transportation.

From the roads south of Baltimore there is certainly but little ground to expect much better results in the future than in the past, nor can we give any encouragement for hope that the common stock of the Philadelphia and Erie will in many years have any value.

(4.) We have strongly stated our anticipations of future profit from the lease of the United Railroads of New Jersey, and given you our reasons therefor. Such an outlet to the city and bay of New York was a necessity, to enable the Company to use its western roads to the best advantage and profit, and to develop the business of its main line and branches.

From your main line and branches there must be, with judicious management in developing the local trade and travel, the production of iron and steel, the mining of coal, and the varied industries of those portions of the State affected by the Company, a constant and valuable increase of business. We have given you some remarkable results of the past history of your main line—showing you that with reduced cost of operating, the road, owing to many causes, has been able largely to reduce the rates of freight, and that for every million of dollars invested in the road in ten years, from 1864 to 1873, inclusive, you have received an annual profit of $282,000; and that with the same elements in the calculation, every million of dollars hereafter invested on the line between New York and Pittsburg, until the business of your road increases seventy-five per cent. above that of 1873, will yield $430,342 per year.

(5.) We have given you a full account of the anthracite coal lands held by your Company; but your investments in this kind of property are of such recent date that we cannot predict the results—time only will develop the wisdom of the policy and its results to your road.

To give you a truer conception of the extent of the influence you exert over the railways of the United States, and of the responsibility you have assumed, we have given you the total mileage and capital involved in the railroads and canals you directly control—showing that it amounts to $5933\frac{6}{10}$ miles, or $7\frac{8}{10}$ per cent. of the whole railroad mileage of the United States, and represents in capital $398,267,675.22, or a fraction less than thirteen per cent. of the whole capital invested in railroads in the United States, and the encouraging fact that the net earnings of all the lines you control and are directly interested in have averaged 6.39 per cent. profit on the whole amount of capital.

We need not suggest to any thoughtful mind what an immense responsibility rests on you from the control of so much capital, nor how fearfully any mismanagement on your part would affect the credit of the country and the support and comfort of the large number of people of every grade and class who are interested in the stocks and bonds of these various companies.

(6.) We have entered very fully into a discussion of the mooted question of the use of your road by the cars of private persons or corporations, and have given our reasons and conclusions, that it is to your interest to encourage such use of your road, and that in obtaining a fair proportion of competitive freight from and to points west of Pittsburg, the use of an intermediate third party is indispensable,—the management being careful to obtain the best possible remuneration from the traffic carried.

(7.) We have discussed very fully the past financial policy of your Company, which led to whatever of loss of credit, inconvenience, or embarrassment your Company has experienced. We have shown you that the true policy of disposing of all securities not absolutely necessary to be held, when even an approximately fair price could have been obtained, has not only not been adopted, but the policy has heretofore been to retain possession of those securities for advanced prices, and to borrow money by issuing stock and bonds to enable you to carry these investments. That if $35,000,000 of these securities had been sold, and which would have brought fair prices in 1872 and 1873, there would have been no necessity for issuing the large amount of stock and selling so many bonds in the latter year. It would practically have saved an increase of your capital stock and funded debt to the value of the securities sold. In consequence of which your Directors were forced to ask for and create the consolidated mortgage, and most unwisely pledged in it securities to the value of $50,000,000.

We have further shown you how this act of July 1st, 1873, was quickly followed by the panic of September, and your Directors were left without available means to meet their wants, how the credit of the Company was injured, and very many of its stockholders seriously affected.

We have carefully considered the financial position of your Company, and have made several recommendations involving questions of floating debt, construction account, reduction of capital, and the general principle of the rigid application of these securities to improvements and betterments, as provided for in the mortgage, and the remainder as they may be or become available, to the purchase and cancellation of bonds issued under that mortgage.

(8.) In examining the policy of the relations heretofore existing between the shareholders and the Directors, and with the view of removing the many causes of distrust and doubt that prevail as to the permanent value of railway securities, and to place responsibility and power where it properly belongs, and to increase the efficiency of the executive officers of the Board, we have made recommendations involving substantial changes in the old plan of organization, which will restore to the shareholders the powers which of right belong to them; and in this connection, we have recommended that hereafter all legislative powers shall be expressly reserved to the shareholders, and executive functions only be given to the Directors. We have shown what these reserved and delegated powers are, and have embodied in resolutions the important features or points, and, therefore, need not repeat them here.

(9.) We have shown that, taking a comprehensive view of the whole operations and obligations of the Pennsylvania Railroad Company, and leaving entirely out of the question the prudence or wisdom of the acts of the past, it reveals a condition of safety which should be very satisfactory to the shareholders; and with, in the future, a more intelligent and active interest on the part of the shareholders and prudent management by the Directors and officers, the Company will offer in its stocks and bonds a safe investment to people of all classes, and will be enabled to fulfill its high duties to the public who use your works, to the city of Philadelphia, and to the power that gave it life—the State of Pennsylvania.

ARTICLE XIII.

Conclusion.

That the Pennsylvania Railroad Company is wonderfully fulfilling the objects of its creation no one can doubt who will compare the comparatively feeble, doubtful, and undeveloped condition of the State of Pennsylvania in 1846, when the Company was chartered, with its present powerful and prosperous position. The Company, by its aid to western lines, has given the city of Pittsburg with its great manufacturing interests an impetus and growth it would not have had depending on the waters of the Ohio. By the opening of the gas-coal mines of Westmoreland and Allegheny counties, the soft coals of Cambria, of Clearfield, and of Huntingdon, the development of the iron interests, the utilization of remote forests, and the immense production of oil, the road has made a home market for the products of the farm, the forest, and the mines all along its lines, and is gathering into the State a rapidly-increasing, sturdy, and energetic population.

The city of Philadelphia has received new life, has sprung into activity, and is rapidly growing from the impulse which the operations of this great line has given her.

The Company is enriching the counties in the State of Pennsylvania, which it reaches by its main line and branches north and west, as well as the cities of Pittsburg and Philadelphia.

With all these benefits conferred on others, it has paid its stockholders from 1853, when the line was opened to Pittsburg, down to 1873,—a period of twenty years,—an average of nine and nine-tenths per cent., the total dividends from its organization to the 1st of January of this year having been two hundred and thirty-four per cent., and the Company stands now, notwithstanding all the losses which we have fully stated, stronger than at any former period, and holding a commanding position in reference to all rival roads and the means of the indefinite development and expansion of the inestimable resources with which Providence has blessed our State—the only one in the Union which commands the connections of the sea, the lakes, and the Mississippi, and possesses within her own borders all the elements of material prosperity.

Your committee, when accepting their appointment, thought they appreciated the extent and importance of their duties; but after entering on the investigation it was soon evident to them that their inquiries, to be satisfactory to you, must take a wider range than the immediate pecuniary questions.

We felt compelled to examine questions of policy as to your relations with other roads and interests, the management of your finances, and the organization of your Company, which demanded the most careful investigation and consideration. We have, therefore, endeavored fully and fearlessly to investigate all these questions, that we might as succinctly as possible present such information as would enable each stockholder to form an estimate of the value of his property, of the true policy by which the Company should in the future be controlled, and of the character of the organization that will most successfully manage their great interests. We believe that the adoption of the various resolutions we offer for your approval will secure, to a great extent, these most desirable results.

In less than thirty years the Company has grown from its small beginnings in 1846, with a capital of $4,000,000, to a corporation controlling thousands of miles of railway and hundreds of millions of capital, second only to the Government in its immediate effects on the people, and closely affecting the interests of the citizens of eleven States of the Union.

We regret the delay in making this report, but it was absolutely unavoidable, unless by such superficial and imperfect examination as would have been a virtual violation of duty in us, and to you wholly unsatisfactory.

Throughout our investigations we have kept steadily in view the point on which we unanimously resolved from the beginning, namely, that our examination should be exhaustive as to subjects, and candid in conclusions. We are far from assuming that we have been able to reach, in all respects, the objects of our aim; but we have done all that we could, and now submit the voluminous results of long labor, over complications hitherto considered incomprehensible to the judgment of stockholders.

> WILL. A. STOKES, *Chairman*,
> W. H. KEMBLE,
> A. LOUDON SNOWDEN,
> D. E. SMALL,
> JNO. S. IRICK,
> WM. C. LONGSTRETH,
> JOHN A. WRIGHT.

ARTICLE XIV.

RESOLUTIONS.

In order that the practical operations of this Company may be most successfully managed, its general interests most carefully protected, and its agents instructed in their proper duties, as well as to vindicate our just authority in the control of our own interests, we, the stockholders of the Pennsylvania Railroad Company, do hereby resolve:—

1. That, as the source of all authority in the premises, we reserve to ourselves the whole legislative power of the corporation which is involved in determining the general policy of the Company; the acceptance or refusal of all laws, whether general or special, of the General Assembly of the State of Pennsylvania which may affect our property, rights, or interests; all assumption of liabilities, either as to the leasing of railroads, guaranteeing the payment of the interest or principal of the bonds or other obligations of any other company; guaranteeing of another company's faithful performance of contract; or in any way binding the Company by obligations for or to other railroad corporations, other than in the ordinary course of contracts required to be made for the proper management of the business of the road; and all other powers not hereinafter expressly committed to the Directors and Officers.

2. That we confide to the wisdom and discretion of the Directors the executive functions of carrying out the

policy, established from time to time by the shareholders, for managing the interests of the Company to the best possible advantage of its stockholders and of the people of this State and of the country, as far as they may be affected by their action, within the powers committed to them.

3. That to enable them to do this the more perfectly, and to secure the necessary intelligence, independence, and responsibility in the board for the good performance of their very responsible duties, we further instruct the Directors to procure the passage of a general law by the General Assembly of the State of Pennsylvania, providing for the election of Directors by the stockholders of a railroad company, who may receive pay for their services, whenever judicial decisions may have so determined the intent and meaning of the seventeenth article of the New Constitution, that it contains nothing prejudicial to the interests of the Company, or whenever for other reasons the Company may accept any general or special law of the Legislature of the State of Pennsylvania, bringing the Company under and subject to the said seventeenth article. Such law, if obtained, to be submitted to the stockholders for their approval at the next following annual meeting.

4. That if such an act is obtained and accepted by the stockholders of the Pennsylvania Railroad Company, there shall thereafter be selected from among the Directors elected by the stockholders at each annual meeting, four persons, three of whom shall be skilled in the construction or management of railways, and one of distinguished reputation for financial experience and skill,—one of the above-named three shall be elected as President of the Company,—the details of duties being left to the discretion of the Directors as a body.

5. That to secure the nomination of suitable and properly qualified persons for the office of Directors, there shall be appointed at each annual meeting, as it may determine, a committee of seven stockholders of the Company, who shall select and nominate, after conferring with the President, ten persons, due regard being had to their qualifications, for the office of Directors for the ensuing year; and that, until the passage and acceptance of an act as above described, it shall be the further duty of said committee, after conferring with the President, to select the proper persons, not exceeding four in number, who shall be recommended for election by the Directors as Vice-Presidents, in accordance with the present law, and that said committee shall publish the names of the persons so selected in not less than five daily newspapers of the city of Philadelphia for six days previous to the day of election of such Directors.

6. That in order that the stockholders may have time to examine the annual report, the Directors shall annually hereafter publish such report in at least three daily newspapers of the city of Philadelphia, one week before each annual meeting, and that such report shall be full and complete, embracing a statement of all the facts and results necessary to enable the stockholders to form a proper estimate of the value of their property and a correct judgment of the ability with which their interests have been taken care of by the Directors. That report shall include, not only the operations of the main line and branches of the Pennsylvania Railroad, and of all railroads leased and operated by this Company, but a sufficiently extended notice of the operations of all the railroads which this Company directly or indirectly controls.

7. That it shall further be the duty of the Board of Directors, at least annually, and oftener if required, or

necessary, to recommend to the stockholders the adoption of such policy or such measures as in their judgment will promote the interests of the Company, with their reasons therefor. That they shall submit with each annual report, or oftener if required, for the approval of the shareholders, estimates for any extraordinary payments or expenses to be made or incurred on the main line or lines leased and directly operated by your Company, and recommend how the money shall be raised to pay for the same.

8. That they shall, at the time of making a semi-annual dividend, or at the intermediate six months of their fiscal year, publish a statement showing the gross receipts, expenses, and net revenues of the main line and branches of the Company operated by it, and showing the amount of net revenue applicable to a dividend.

9. That the credit of this Company may be protected, the Directors are prohibited from incurring any floating debts in the form of bills payable or acceptances, except to meet, and then only for temporary use, expenses for improvements, enlargements, or betterments on the main line and the railroads of the United Companies of New Jersey; and are also prohibited, except by special permission of the stockholders, from loaning the credit of this Company to other companies, excepting such as may own roads controlled by this Company by lease or stock ownership. And further, that all powers or authority heretofore given to the board, so far as they conflict with the language or the spirit of this resolution, are hereby revoked and annulled.

AND WHEREAS, The shareholders of the Pennsylvania Railroad Company are convinced that the placing of securities to the value of $50,000,000 in the consolidated mortgage was unnecessary to give perfect security to the bonds to be issued under that mortgage, and that they do not add to the facility of sale nor to the marketable value of such bonds, and that the mortgage provides for bonds largely beyond any present prospective wants of the Company, and as their presence in this mortgage operates as a bar against the true policy of this Company, viz., the reduction of the amount of bonded indebtedness and the payment of the floating debt: therefore

Resolved, That the Directors be and are hereby instructed—

1. That the policy of the Company hereafter, in its relations to other companies now controlled by it, shall be—in all cases where it is important for the interests of the Pennsylvania Railroad Company—either to consolidate or effect leases on just terms to both parties, giving the preference to the plan so successfully adopted in many instances by your Company, of leasing roads to be worked at cost, thereby avoiding many complications, and further relieving your treasury from the necessity of holding large amounts of securities, which they are now compelled to keep, in order to retain control of the roads, thus at once releasing securities to the value of many millions of dollars which should be applied as hereinafter recommended.

2. That the Directors be and are hereby instructed to conform rigidly to the provisions of the consolidated mortgage by appropriating the proceeds of such securities as are available for sale to the payment of all betterments, improvements, and real estate purchases, for the benefit of the mortgaged premises.

3. That the Directors shall, from time to time, sell such available securities as may not be required to pay for betterments, &c., as above, the proceeds whereof shall be invested

in the bonds of the Company, that they may be canceled and the remaining securities the sooner released from the lien of the mortgages.

4. That in our opinion, the policy above established will render unnecessary any further issue of bonds under that mortgage, without the formal approval of the stockholders first had and obtained, except the £5,000,000 already issued, or arranged to be issued, and the bonds appropriated under the mortgage to pay off existing bonds as they mature.

AND WHEREAS, The interests of your Company may be unfavorably affected by the presence of other stockholders in the Pennsylvania Company: therefore

Resolved, That we recommend to the Directors to adopt such measures as will, in their judgment, secure to the Pennsylvania Railroad Company the absolute and exclusive control of the policy of the Pennsylvania Company.

The above preamble and resolutions are respectfully recommended to the favorable consideration and action of the stockholders.

WILL. A. STOKES, *Chairman*,
W. H. KEMBLE,
A. LOUDON SNOWDEN,
D. E. SMALL,
JNO. S. IRICK,
WM. C. LONGSTRETH,
JOHN A. WRIGHT.

APPENDIX A.

List of Stocks owned by the Pennsylvania Railroad Company December 31st, 1873.

Par.	No. of Shares.	Name of Security.	Par.	Per Share.	Cash Value.
$2,075,000	41,500	Allegheny Valley Railroad stock,	$50	$10 00	$415,000
400,000	4,000	American Steamship stock, . . .	100	20 00	80,000
184,100	3,682	Bald Eagle Valley Railroad stock,	50	50 00	184,100
1,828,600	36,572	Baltimore and Potomac Railroad stock, ...	50	1 00	36,572
308,950	6,179	Bedford and Bridgeport Railroad stock, ...	50	1 00	6,179
325,000	6,500	Chartiers Railway stock, ...	50	10 00	65,000
1,100,000	22,000	Cleveland, Mt. Vernon and Delaware Railroad stock, common,	50	1 00	22,000
290,100	5,802	Cleveland, Mt. Vernon and Delaware Railroad stock, preferred,	50	40 00	232,000
1,277,350	25,547	Connecting Railway stock, six per cent. guaranteed, ...	50	50 00	1,277,350
132,150	5,286	Cresson Springs stock, ...	25	. . .	50,000
237,200	4,744	Cumberland Valley Railroad stock, preferred, ...	50	60 00	284,640
975,800	19,516	Cumberland Valley Railroad stock, common, ...	50	60 00	1,170,960
762,550	15,251	Harrisburg and Lancaster Railroad stock, ...	50	50 00	762,550
56,500	1,130	Junction Railroad stock, ...	50	50 00	56,500
1,921,700	19,217	Jeffersonville, Madison and Indianapolis Railroad stock, . . .	100	85 50	1,643,400
281,200	5,624	Little Miami Railroad stock, . .	50	50 00	281,200
7,480	374	Lewistown and Tuscarora Bridge Company stock, ...	20	2 00	5,000
375,900	3,759	Louisville Bridge stock, ...	100	100 00	375,900
302,000	6,040	Lykens Valley Coal stock, . . .	50	. . .	395,765
720,000	7,200	Newport and Cincinnati Bridge stock, ...	100	7 50	108,000
25,000	250	New Jersey Stock-Yard and Market Company stock, ...	100	80 00	20,000
$13,586,580	. . .	. . . Carried forward, . . .	. .	. . .	$7,472,116

Par.	No. of Shares.	Name of Security.	Par.	Per Share.	Cash Value.
$13,586,580	. . . .	. . . Brought forward, . . .	. .	. . .	$7,472,116
2,421,000	48,420	Northern Central Railway Company stock, ...	$50	$40 00	1,936,800
3,511,550	70,231	Pennsylvania Canal stock, . . .	50	15 00	1,053,465
8,000,000	160,000	Pennsylvania Company preferred stock, ...	50	50 00	8,000,000
2,049,200	40,984	Pennsylvania Railroad stock, . .	50	50 00	2,049,200
679,800	6,798	Pennsylvania Steel Company stock, ...	100	75 00	509,850
1,581,800	31,636	Philadelphia and Erie Railroad common stock, ... - .	50	. . .	. . . . .
2,400,000	48,000	Philadelphia and Erie Railroad preferred stock, ...	50	10 00	480,000
1,250	250	Philadelphia and Merion Railroad stock, one installment only paid, ...	. .	5 00	1,250
10,000	80	Philadelphia and Southern Mail Steamship stock, ...	125	37 50	3,000
3,000,000	60,000	Pittsburg, Cincinnati and St. Louis Railway preferred stock,	50	. . .	. . . . .
1,280,000	12,800	Pittsburg, Fort Wayne and Chicago Railway special seven per cent. guaranteed stock, .	100	90 00	1,152,000
5,100	51	Pittsburg, Fort Wayne and Chicago Railway common stock, .	100	85 00	3,315
405,000	8,100	Pittsburg, Virginia and Charleston Railway stock, ...	50	40 00	324,000
123,300	1,233	Pullman Palace Car stock, . . .	100	100 00	123,300
275,000	5,500	South West Pennsylvania Railroad stock, ...	50	37 50	206,250
1,252,400	25,048	Summit Branch Railroad stock, .	50	45 00	1,127,160
1,000,000	10,000	Susquehanna Coal Company stock	100	100 00	1,000,000
508,800	10,176	Tyrone and Clearfield Railroad stock, ...	50	50 00	508,800
124,900	2,498	West Chester and Philadelphia Railroad preferred stock, . . .	50	50 00	124,900
972,650	19,453	Western Pennsylvania Railroad stock, ...	50	50 00	972,650
54,285	1,551	West Jersey Railroad stock, second and third installments, . .	50	50 00	54,285
317,050	6,341	Wrightsville, York and Gettysburg Railroad stock, ...	50	. . .	170,541
981,575	39,263	Shamokin Coal Company stock, .	25	10 00	392,630
$44,541,240					$27,665,512

*List of Bonds owned by the Pennsylvania Railroad Company
December 31st, 1873.*

Par.	Name of Security.	Rate per cent.	Cash Value.
$8,500	Allegheny County bonds, "Pennsylvania Railroad loan," six per cent,	100	$8,500
2,000	Allegheny County bonds, "P. & S. loan," six per cent.,	75	1,500
512,000	Alexandria and Fredericksburg Railway first mortgage bonds, seven per cent., gold,	70	358,400
3,959,000	Allegheny Valley Railroad first mortgage seven per cent. bonds,	85	3,365,150
29,100	Bald Eagle Valley Railroad first mortgage six per cent. bonds,	85	24,735
100,000	Bald Eagle Valley Railroad second mortgage seven per cent. bonds,	90	90,000
1,000,000	Bedford and Bridgeport Railroad first mortgage seven per cent. bonds,	80	800,000
300,000	Central Stock Yard and Transit Company seven per cent. bonds,	90	270,000
50,000	City of Altoona "Water loan," seven and three-tenths per cent. bonds,	90	45,000
4,600	City of Harrisburg "Water loan," six per cent. bonds,	90	4,140
752,000	Cincinnati and Muskingum Valley Railroad first mortgage seven per cent. bonds,	70	526,400
1,000,000	Columbia and Port Deposit Railroad bonds,	60	600,000
1,258,000	Columbus, Chicago and Indiana Central Railway second mortgage, $5,000,000 loan, seven per cent. bonds,	70	880,600
3,504,000	Columbus, Chicago and Indiana Central Railway, $10,000,000 loan, seven per cent. income bonds,	50	1,752,000
15,000	County of Clark, Illinois, eight per cent. bonds,	75	11,250
264,000	Danville, Hazleton and Wilkesbarre Railroad first mortgage seven per cent. bonds,	60	158,400
112,900	East Brandywine and Waynesburg Railroad first mortgage seven per cent. bonds,	75	84,675
3,600	East Brandywine and Waynesburg Railroad, New Holland Extension,	75	2,700
100,000	Erie and Pittsburg Railroad seven per cent. bonds,	80	80,000
20,000	Holliday's Cove Railroad second mortgage seven per cent. bonds,	100	20,000
19,000	Huntingdon and Broad Top Railroad and Coal Company consolidated mortgage bonds,	40	7,600
$13,013,700	. . . . Carried forward, ...	. .	$9,091,050

Par.	Name of Security.	Rate per cent.	Cash Value.
$13,013,700	.... Brought forward, ...	..	$9,091,050
440,000	Indianapolis and St. Louis Railroad first mortgage seven per cent. bonds, ...	90	396,000
50,000	Indianapolis and St. Louis Railroad equipment bonds, ...	90	45,000
350,000	International Navigation Company first mortgage bonds, ...	90	315,000
271,000	Jersey City and Bergen Railroad first mortgage seven per cent. bonds, ...	90	243,900
9,000	Lawrence Railroad first mortgage bonds, ...	90	8,100
1,500,000	Lewisburg, Centre and Spruce Creek Railroad first mortgage seven per cent. bonds, ...	75	1,125,000
200,000	Mifflin and Centre County Railroad first mortgage six per cent. bonds, ...	50	100,000
1,200,000	Newport and Cincinnati Bridge bonds, ...	85	1,020,000
1,000,000	Northern Central Railway seven per cent. income bonds, convertible, ...	85	850,000
2,000	Ohio and Pennsylvania Bridge seven per cent. bonds, ...	100	2,000
18,000	Pennsylvania Canal bonds, ...	60	10,800
3,111,000	Pennsylvania Company first mortgage seven per cent. bonds, gold, ...	85	2,644,350
3,000	Pennsylvania Railroad first mortgage bonds, ...	100	3,000
1,000	Pennsylvania Railroad second mortgage bonds, ..	100	1,000
1,000	Philadelphia and Erie Railroad six per cent. bonds, currency, ...	80	800
729,000	Philadelphia and Erie Railroad six per cent. bonds, gold, ...	80	583,200
500,000	Pittsburg, Virginia and Charleston Railway seven per cent. gold bonds, ...	80	400,000
770,000	Pullman Palace Car eight per cent. bonds, ...	100	770,000
1,024,000	Shamokin Valley and Pottsville Railroad six per cent. gold bonds, ...	90	912,600
6,000	South Mountain Iron Company bonds, ...	75	4,500
278,000	Steubenville and Indiana Railroad seven per cent. bonds, ...	75	208,500
5,000	St. Louis and Iron Mountain Railway seven per cent. bonds, ...	75	3,750
225,000	St. Louis, Vandalia and Terre Haute Railroad second mortgage convertible bonds, ...	70	157,500
700,000	St. Louis, Vandalia and Terre Haute Railroad seven per cent. income bonds, ...	50	350,000
$25,406,700	.... Carried forward, ...	..	$19,246,050

Par.	Name of Security.	Rate per cent.	Cash Value.
$25,406,700	. . . . Brought forward, ...	. .	$19,246,050
900,000	Toledo, Tiffin and Eastern Railroad seven per cent. gold bonds, ...	70	630,000
292,500	Warren and Franklin Railroad first mortgage seven per cent. bonds, ...	75	219,375
1,200,000	Western Pennsylvania Railroad general mortgage seven per cent. bonds, ...	90	1,080,000
10,000	Western Pennsylvania Railroad first mortgage six per cent. bonds, ...	85	8,500
148,000	Western Pennsylvania Railroad six per cent. branch bonds, ... Western Pennsylvania Railroad six per cent. branch bonds, ... Western Pennsylvania Railroad six per cent. branch bonds, ...	85	125,800
15,000	West Chester and Philadelphia Railroad first mortgage seven per cent. bonds, ...	100	15,000
52,000	Wrightsville, York and Gettysburg Railroad six per cent. bonds, ...	100	52,000
1,029,000	Pittsburg, Cincinnati and St. Louis Railway consolidated mortgage bonds, ...	65	668,850
$29,053,200			$22,045,575

A Statement

Of the Liabilities and Operations of the Corporations whose Stocks or Bonds are held by the Pennsylvania Railroad Company, Showing the Basis on which the Appraisements were made, with Explanatory Notes.

CONNECTING RAILROAD.		Par Value.	Total Par Value.	Assessed Value.	Total Assessed Value.
This road was originally leased to the Philadelphia and Trenton Railroad, sublet to the Pennsylvania Railroad. This sum represents the entire capital stock. The road is substantially a part of the main line of the Pennsylvania Railroad. *Held by Pennsylvania Railroad Company:*					
Capital stock, six per cent.,	$1,277,350 00	$50	$1,277,350	. . .	$1,277,350
JUNCTION RAILROAD.					
Capital stock,	$185,000 00				
Bonded debt,	800,000 00				
Floating debt,	26,340 00				
Held by Pennsylvania Railroad Company:					
Capital stock,	$56,500 00	$50	$56,500	. . .	$56,500
Net earnings for 1873, (equal to a dividend of eight per cent.,)	63,733 00				

Connects the Pennsylvania Railroad with the Philadelphia, Wilmington and Baltimore Railroad and Reading Railroad.

HARRISBURG, PORTSMOUTH, MT. JOY AND LANCASTER RAILROAD.		Par Value.	Total Par Value.	Assessed Value.	Total Assessed Value.
Leased to Pennsylvania Railroad Company, and a part of the main line extending from Lancaster to Harrisburg. Annual rental, interest on bonds and seven per cent. on capital stock.					
Held by Pennsylvania Railroad Company:					
Capital stock,	$762,550 00	$50	$762,550	. . .	$762,550

	Par Value.	Total Par Value.	Assessed Value.	Total Assessed Value.
East Brandywine and Waynesburg Railroad.				
Capital stock, ... $133,351 45				
Bonded debt—				
First mortgage bonds, seven per cent., . . . 140,000 00				
Second mortgage bonds, seven per cent., . . . 135,000 00				
Held by Pennsylvania Railroad Company:				
First mortgage bonds, seven per cent., . . . $112,900 00	$500 / 100	$112,900	. . .	$84,675
Extension bonds, . . . 3,600 00	100	3,600	. . .	2,700
Net earnings for 1873, . 7,018 61				
Wrightsville, York and Gettysburg Railroad.				
This road has been purchased by the Pennsylvania Railroad Company and made a part of their road.				
Held by Pennsylvania Railroad Company:				
Stock, ... $317,050 00	$50	$317,050	. . .	$222,541
Bonds, ... 52,000 00	1,000	52,000		
Costing, ... $222,541 00				
Columbia and Port Deposit Railroad.				
First mortgage bonds, seven per cent., (all held by Pennsylvania Railroad Company,) . $1,000,000 00	$1,000	$1,000,000	. . .	$600,000

This is an extension of the line along the east bank of the Susquehanna, from Harrisburg to tide-water, and is to form an extension of the Low-Grade for the movement of heavy traffic. Part of this line is in operation, and work progressing slowly upon the remainder.

CUMBERLAND VALLEY RAILROAD.		Par Value.	Total Par Value.	Assessed Value.	Total Assessed Value.
Bonded debt,	$435,857 00				
Preferred and common stock,	1,774,912 00				
	$2,210,769 00				
Net earnings for 1873, (a sum equal to its interest and fifteen per cent. on its capital stock,)	$294,743 00				
This road has a sinking fund of $867,134 set aside from its surplus earnings.					
Held by Pennsylvania Railroad Company:					
Preferred stock, eight per cent.,	$237,200 00	$50	$237,200	. . .	$260,920
Common stock, eight per cent.,	975,800 00	50	975,800	. . .	1,073,380
Eight per cent. dividend declared.					
NORTHERN CENTRAL RAILWAY.					
Capital stock,	$5,842,000 00				
Bonded debt,	11,419,756 00				
Floating debt,	1,599,923 00				
Net earnings for 1873, (equal to a dividend on capital stock of four and one-quarter per cent.,)	1,583,581 00				
Included in expenses are $215,852 extraordinary expenditures.					
Held by Pennsylvania Railroad Company:					
Capital stock,	$2,421,000 00	$50	$2,421,000	. . .	$1,694,700
Income bonds, seven per cent.,	1,000,000 00	1,000	1,000,000	. . .	850,000
SHAMOKIN VALLEY AND POTTSVILLE RAILROAD.					
Leased to Northern Central Railway Company at six per cent. on stock and interest on bonded debt.					
Bonded debt—					
First mortgage bonds, seven per cent,	$700,000 00				
Second mortgage bonds, seven per cent.,	1,288,000 00				
Held by Pennsylvania Railroad Company:					
Second mortgage bonds,	$1,024,000 00	$1,000 500	$1,024,000	. . .	$912,600

	Par Value.	Total Par Value.	Assessed Value.	Total Assessed Value.
DANVILLE, HAZLETON AND WILKESBARRE RAILROAD.				
Leased to Pennsylvania Railroad Company at cost, with a proviso that the Pennsylvania Railroad will advance sufficient moneys to the purchase of coupons as shall meet the interest on its bonded debt; and should the net earnings be insufficient to liquidate any portion of the coupons, the Pennsylvania Railroad will not foreclose until the expiration of the lease. Terms of lease, thirty-three years from 1872. Income for 1873 not sufficient to pay interest on bonded debt.				
Capital stock, ... $684,235 00				
Bonded debt, seven per cent., ... 1,400,000 00				
Floating debt, ... 160,000 00				
Held by Pennsylvania Railroad Company:				
First mortgage bonds, seven per cent., . . $264,000 00	$1,000 500 200	$264,000	. . .	$158,400
BALD EAGLE VALLEY RAILROAD.				
Leased to Pennsylvania Railroad at forty per cent. of gross receipts.				
Capital stock, ... $550,000 00				
First mortgage bonds, six per cent., ... 354,900 00				
Second mortgage convertible bonds, seven per cent., ... 100,000 00				
Held by Pennsylvania Railroad Company:				
Capital stock, ... $184,100 00	$50	$184,100	. . .	$184,100
First mortgage bonds, . 29,100 00	1,000 500 100	29,100	. . .	24,735
Second mortgage bonds, 100,000 00	100	100,000	. . .	90,000
Net earnings for 1873, (equal to a dividend of eleven per cent.,) . . 89,488 15				

Tyrone and Clearfield Railroad.		Par Value.	Total Par Value.	Assessed Value.	Total Assessed Value.
Capital stock,	$510,000 00				
Floating debt,	313,566 98				
Held by Pennsylvania Railroad Company:					
Capital stock,	$508,800 00	$50	$508,800	. . .	$508,800
Net earnings for 1873, (equal to a dividend of eight and one-half per cent.,)	62,244 35				

Mifflin and Centre County Railroad.					
Capital stock,	$65,675 00				
First mortgage bonds, six per cent.,	200,000 00				
Loss for 1873,	13,382 59				
Held by Pennsylvania Railroad Company:					
First mortgage bonds, six per cent.,	$200,000 00	$1,000 500	$200,000	. . .	$100,000

These bonds were taken to aid the construction of a branch from Lewistown to Milroy, and are the first mortgage on that line.

Bedford and Bridgeport Railroad.		Par Value.	Total Par Value.	Assessed Value.	Total Assessed Value.
Capital stock,	$356,952 00				
First mortgage bonds, seven per cent.,	1,000,000 00				
Loss for 1873,	3,252 72				
Held by Pennsylvania Railroad Company:					
Capital stock,	$308,950 00	$50	$308,950	. . .	$6,179
First mortgage bonds, seven per cent.,	1,000,000 00	1,000	1,000,000	. . .	800,000

These bonds were taken to aid the construction of the line from the terminus of the Huntingdon and Broad Top Railroad to Bedford Springs and the Cumberland coal region and the city of Cumberland. (See the statement as to stock of that company.)

Huntingdon and Broad Top Railroad.		Par Value.	Total Par Value.	Assessed Value.	Total Assessed Value.
Held by Pennsylvania Railroad Company:					
Consolidated seven per cent. bonds,	$19,000 00	$1,000	$19,000	. . .	$7,600

Road in the hands of trustees, who hope, after October, 1874, to permanently resume paying interest on entire indebtedness.

South Western Pennsylvania Railroad.	Par Value.	Total Par Value.	Assessed Value.	Total Assessed Value.
Capital stock, ... $359,857 50				
Floating debt, ... 590,815 86				
Held by Pennsylvania Railroad Company:				
Capital stock, ... $275,000 00	$50	$275,000	. . .	$206,250
Net earnings, 1873, . . 56,746 98				

The officers of the Pennsylvania Railroad report as follows:—This stock represents the control of the road from Greensburg to Connellsville, which was built to secure a share of the large coke trade, which forms an important item of traffic over our western lines to Chicago, Cleveland, Indianapolis, and other points. It is deemed to be the best coke manufactured from any coal deposit now known.

Western Pennsylvania Railroad.	Par Value.	Total Par Value.	Assessed Value.	Total Assessed Value.
Extends from Blairsville to Butler. Leased to Pennsylvania Railroad Company at cost.				
Capital stock, ... $1,022,450 00				
Bonds—First mortgage, main line, six per cent, 800,000 00				
Bonds—First mortgage, Pittsburg Branch, six per cent., ... 1,000,000 00				
Bonds—General mortgage, seven per cent., 1,200,000 00				
Total, ... $4,022,450 00				
Floating debt, ... $180,847 20				
Net earnings, 1873, . . 348,968 77				
Amount required to pay interest, ... 192,000 00				
Balance, (equal to fifteen and one-third per cent. on its capital stock,) . $156,968 77				
Held by Pennsylvania Railroad Company:				
First mortgage bonds, six per cent., ... $10,000 00	$1,000	$10,000	. . .	$8,500
Branch bonds, six per cent., ... 148,000 00	1,000 / 500 / 100	148,000	. . .	125,800
General mortgage bonds, seven per cent., . . 1,200,000 00	1,000	1,200,000	. . .	1,080,000
Capital stock, ... 972,650 00	50	972,650	. . .	972,650

Lewisburg, Centre and Spruce Creek Railroad.				
Leased to Pennsylvania Railroad Co. at cost.				
Capital stock, ... $245,635 00				
First mortgage bonds, seven per cent., . . 1,545,000 00				
Held by Pennsylvania Railroad Company:				
First mortgage bonds, seven per cent., . . $1,500,000 00	$1,000	$1,500,000	. . .	$1,125,000
Net earnings, 1873, . . 6,983 94				

These bonds were taken by the Company to aid the construction of the road from Lewisburg, Union county, Pennsylvania, and form a connection from the Philadelphia and Erie Railroad through to Tyrone, Blair county. A portion of the line is fully constructed and in operation, and a portion of the residue graded. A very small amount of work is being done on the road at present.

PITTSBURG, VIRGINIA AND CHARLESTON RAILWAY.		Par Value.	Total Par Value.	Assessed Value.	Total Assessed Value.
Capital stock,	$673,264 31				
Bonded and other debt,	1,264,138 53				
Total,	$1,937,402 84				
Receipts for 1873,	$67,137 11				
Expenses for 1873,	41,558 18				
Net earnings for 1873,	$25,578 93				
Held by Pennsylvania Railroad Company:					
Capital stock,	$405,000 00	$50	$405,000	. . .	$324,000
Seven per cent. gold bonds,	500,000 00	1,000	500,000	. . .	400,000

A new enterprise not yet finished, but using such portions as are finished. Extends from Pittsburg to Monongahela City.

Its value can best be explained by the subjoined statement of the officers of the Pennsylvania Railroad:—"This stock was taken with the view of securing a connection from the Pittsburg, Cincinnati and St. Louis Railway, at the south end of the Monongahela bridge, at Pittsburg, to our main line east of Turtle Creek; the purpose being to make a transfer depot between the south-western roads and our main line, at Wall's station, sixteen miles east of Pittsburg, thus avoiding the crossing of the river into Pittsburg, the tunnel, and the already over-crowded yards in the city, and, also, the lifting over the grades between Pittsburg and Turtle Creek. The line of the Pittsburg, Virginia and Charleston Railway follows the river valley, and when completed will give us great facilities for the south-western trade. A large property has been secured at Wall's station for this purpose, and will be made available as soon as the line is completed."

WARREN AND FRANKLIN RAILROAD.		Par Value.	Total Par Value.	Assessed Value.	Total Assessed Value.
Since merged into Oil Creek and Allegheny River Railroad.					
Held by Pennsylvania Railroad Company:					
First mortgage bonds, seven per cent.,	$292,500 00	$1,000 500	$292,500	. . .	$219,375
Net earnings, double the amount required to pay interest on its first mortgage.					

THE AMERICAN STEAMSHIP COMPANY.		Par Value.	Total Par Value.	Assessed Value.	Total Assessed Value.
Held by Pennsylvania Railroad Company:					
Capital stock,	$400,000 00	$100	$400,000	. . .	$80,000
Deficiency for 1873,	90,000 00				
Net earnings insufficient to pay interest on bonded debt.					

	Par Value.	Total Par Value.	Assessed Value.	Total Assessed Value.
PENNSYLVANIA STEEL COMPANY.				
Capital stock, ... $1,834,560 24				
Bonded debt, ... 198,000 00				
Held by Pennsylvania Railroad Company:				
Capital stock . . . $679,800 00	$100	$679,800	. . .	$509,850
Net earnings, 1873, (equal to a dividend of thirteen and one-half per cent.,) 263,040 50				
CENTRAL STOCK-YARD, JERSEY CITY.				
First mortgage bonds, seven per cent., . . $300,000 00	$1,000	$300,000	. . .	$270,000
Held by Pennsylvania Railroad Company:				
Secured by real estate located in Jersey City, opposite New York City, costing over $600,000.				
JERSEY CITY AND BERGEN RAILROAD.				
Capital stock, ... $110,100 00				
Bonded debt, ... 584,100 00				
Floating debt, ... 393,782 77				
Held by Pennsylvania Railroad Company:				
First mortgage bonds, seven per cent., . . $271,000 00	$1,000	$271,000	. . .	$243,900
Net earnings for 1873, . 41,718 59				
CRESSON SPRINGS.				
Capital stock, ... $138,050 00				
Held by Pennsylvania Railroad Company:				
Capital stock, ... $132,150 00	$25	$132,150	. . .	$50,000
Net earnings for 1873, . 6,552 82				
INTERNATIONAL NAVIGATION COMPANY.				
Held by Pennsylvania Railroad Company:				
First mortgage bonds, seven per cent., . . $350,000 00	$1,000	$350,000	. . .	$315,000
Secured by a mortgage on real estate, in Philadelphia, on which more than double the amount is being spent. A first-class security.				
PENNSYLVANIA CANAL.				
Capital stock, ... $4,458,890 00				
Bonded debt, ... 2,641,000 00				
Floating debt, ... 490,200 00				
Held by Pennsylvania Railroad Company:				
Capital stock, ... $3,511,550 00	$50	$3,511,550	. . .	$1,053,465
Bonds, six per cent., . . 18,000 00	1,000	18,000	. . .	10,800
Net earnings for 1873, . 319,932 32				

MISCELLANEOUS BONDS.	Par Value.	Total Par Value.	Assessed Value.	Total Assessed Value.
Allegheny county bonds, six per cent.,	$1,000 / 500	$8,500	. . .	$8,500
Allegheny county bonds, six per cent.,	1,000	2,000	. . .	1,500
Altoona city bonds, seven and three-tenths per cent.,	1,000	50,000	. . .	45,000
Harrisburg bonds, six per cent.,	1,000 / 500	4,600	. . .	4,140
County of Clark (Illinois) bonds, eight per cent.,	1,000	15,000	. . .	11,250

The above bonds are secured by the real estate of the municipalities issuing them.

PHILADELPHIA AND ERIE RAILROAD.		Par Value.	Total Par Value.	Assessed Value.	Total Assessed Value.
Leased to Pennsylvania Railroad Co. at cost.					
Common stock,	$6,048,700 00				
Preferred stock,	2,400,000 00				
Bonded debt,	16,252,000 00				
Floating debt,	1,335,000 00				
Total,	$26,035,700 00				
Held by Pennsylvania Railroad Company:					
Common stock,	$1,581,800 00	$50	$1,581,800		
Preferred stock,	2,400,000 00	50	2,400,000		
Six per cent. gold bonds,	730,000 00	1,000	730,000	. . .	$584,000
Expenses and interest for 1873,	4,593,327 00				
Receipts and interest for 1873,	3,965,067 00				
Deficit,	$628,260 00				

For a long time the net earnings have been insufficient to pay interest, each yearly loss being met by a further issue of bonds. The liabilities have far outstripped the receipts in their growth. Since 1869 the increase on gross receipts has been seventeen and seven-tenths per cent., and the increase in liabilities thirty-nine and six-tenths per cent. The whole of the increase in liabilities has been in bonded debt and preferred stock. Some hope of its future is entertained by its friends by reason of the connection with the Low-Grade Railroad, at Driftwood, and Buffalo, New York and Philadelphia Railroad, at Emporium. At the present cost of running the road it would require gross receipts amounting to $14,000,000 per annum to yield income sufficient to pay its interest and six per cent. on its capital, an amount so utterly preposterous that no sane person would dare estimate on. A road whose gross receipts has increased but $600,000 in four years, and that, too, as its president estimates, by extraordinary and unprofitable efforts, cannot possibly increase sufficiently fast to overtake its expense and interest account, much less pay a dividend to its common stockholders. The question suggests itself, how long can it remain in the hands of its stockholders? The answer is, "Just as long as the Pennsylvania Railroad is willing to loan it money to meet its deficit, and no longer." In addition to the floating debt above, it is indebted to the Pennsylvania Railroad $2,401,097.36.

WEST JERSEY RAILROAD.		Par Value.	Total Par Value.	Assessed Value.	Total Assessed Value.
Capital stock,	$1,359,750 00				
Bonded debt,	2,400,000 00				
Floating debt,	71,125 00				
Held by Pennsylvania Railroad Company:					
Capital stock,	$54,285 00	$50	$54,285	. . .	$54,285
Net earnings for 1873, after paying interest on its bonded debt,	97,723 83				
ALEXANDRIA AND FREDERICKSBURG RAILWAY.					
Capital stock,	$1,000,000 00				
Bonded debt—					
First mortgage bonds, seven per cent.,(gold,)	1,000,000 00				
Floating debt,	264,053 00				
Held by Pennsylvania Railroad Company:					
First mortgage bonds, seven per cent., (gold,)	$512,000 00	$1,000	$512,000	. . .	$358,400
Operations for 1873 show a loss,	25,074 02				

Now in the hands of trustees for bondholders.

PITTSBURG, FORT WAYNE AND CHICAGO RAILWAY.		Par Value.	Total Par Value.	Assessed Value.	Total Assessed Value.
Held by Pennsylvania Railroad Company:					
Common stock,	$5,100 00	$100	$5,100	. . .	$3,315
Seven per cent. guaranteed stock,	1,280,000 00	100	1,280,000	. . .	1,152,000
Leased to Pennsylvania Railroad Company, and sublet to Pennsylvania Company, at interest and seven per cent. on its stock.					
Operations for 1873—					
Surplus, after paying interest and dividends,	$954,855 00				

	Par Value.	Total Par Value.	Assessed Value.	Total Assessed Value.
PENNSYLVANIA COMPANY.				
Assets, consisting of bonds, stocks, real estate, equipment, bills receivable, cash, and cash items, ... $30,778,109 68				
Liabilities—				
Common stock, . $3,360,900 00				
Preferred stock, . 8,000,000 00				
Mortgage, . . 3,111,000 00				
Floating debt, . 12,008,766 22				
26,480,666 22				
Balance, being undivided profits, ... $4,297,443 46				
Operations for 1873—				
Profits from leased lines, and gross receipts from their own rolling stock, &c., ... 2,534,853 95				
Expense, . . . $32,198 37				
Discount and interest, . . . 430,991 75				
Loss on sale of securities, . . 833,353 47				
1,296,543 59				
Profits for year, (equal to a dividend of ten and nine-tenths per cent. on the entire capital,) $1,238,310 36				
It will be observed that $833,353.47 has been deducted from the profits of this year for loss on sale of securities. It is hardly fair, although showing great prudence, to charge the sum against a single year's earnings.				
Held by Pennsylvania Railroad Company:				
First mortgage bonds, seven per cent., (gold,) $3,111,000 00	$1,000	$3,111,000	. . .	$2,644,350
Guaranteed stock, ... 8,000,000 00	50	8,000,000	. . .	8,000,000

ERIE AND PITTSBURG RAILROAD.		Par Value.	Total Par Value.	Assessed Value.	Total Assessed Value.
Leased to Pennsylvania Railroad Company, and sublet to Pennsylvania Company.					
Rent for 1873, (a sum nearly double the amount required to pay its interest,)	$380,626 00				
Held by Pennsylvania Railroad Company:					
Seven per cent. bonds,	$100,000 00	$1,000	$100,000	. . .	$80,000
Surplus earnings, being profit to Pennsylvania Company, over and above rental,	103,772 74				
LAWRENCE RAILROAD.					
Leased to Pittsburg, Fort Wayne and Chicago Railway Company. Rent for 1873, a sum equal to three times its interest.					
Held by Pennsylvania Railroad Company:					
First mortgage bonds, seven per cent.,	$9,000 00	$1,000	$9,000	. . .	$8,100
Surplus earnings, after paying rental, a profit to Pennsylvania Railroad,	258 00				
TOLEDO, TIFFIN AND EASTERN RAILROAD.					
First mortgage seven per cent. gold bonds,	$900,000 00	$1,000	$900,000	. . .	$630,000

This is a new enterprise now in course of construction.
These bonds were received by this Company for advances made through the Pennsylvania Company to aid the construction of that line.

INDIANAPOLIS AND ST. LOUIS RAILROAD.		Par Value.	Total Par Value.	Assessed Value.	Total Assessed Value.
Extends from Terre Haute to Indianapolis. Leased to Pennsylvania Railroad Company, and sublet to Pennsylvania Company.					
Rent for 1873, (being a sum sufficient to pay interest on all liabilities, and a surplus of $8000,)	$245,259 00				
Held by Pennsylvania Railroad Company:					
First mortgage bonds, seven per cent.,	$440,000 00	$1,000	$440,000	. . .	$396,000
Equipment bonds, seven per cent.,	50,000 00	1,000	50,000	. . .	45,000

JEFFERSONVILLE, MADISON AND INDIANAPOLIS RAILROAD.		Par Value.	Total Par Value.	Assessed Value.	Total Assessed Value.
Length, two hundred and twenty-four miles.					
Capital stock,	$2,000,000 00				
Bonded debt,	4,888,000 00				
	$6,888,000 00				
Held by Pennsylvania Railroad Company:					
Stock, seven per cent. guaranteed,	$1,921,700 00	$100	$1,921,700	. . .	$1,537,360
Leased to Pennsylvania Railroad Company at interest on bonds and seven per cent. on capital stock; sublet to Pennsylvania Company.					
Gross receipts for 1873,	$1,434,993 01				
Expenses for 1873,	991,377 03				
Net profits,	$443,615 98				
Amount required to pay interest and other expenses,	392,651 70				
Balance for stockholders,	$50,964 28				
Amount required to pay dividend on stock,	140,000 00				
Deficiency to be made up by lessee,	$89,035 72				
The above deficiency was made good by Pennsylvania Company, and charged in their statement for 1873 to profit and loss.					
CLEVELAND, MOUNT VERNON AND DELAWARE RAILROAD.					
Capital stock,	$1,300,000 00				
Preferred stock,	451,450 00				
Bonded debt,	2,300,000 00				
Held by Pennsylvania Railroad Company:					
Capital stock,	$1,100,000 00	$50	$1,100,000	. . .	$22,000
Preferred stock,	290,100 00	50	290,100	. . .	232,080

The business of 1873 fell short of interest account $8646. The year 1874 promises, so far, more than sufficient. Considered well for a new enterprise.

The following report of the officers of the Pennsylvania Railroad Company will explain more fully its value:—

These twenty-two thousand shares of common stock came to this Company as a bonus upon the re-organization of that road.

The portion of the line from Hudson to Millersburg, crossing the Fort Wayne road at Orrville, we received in connection with the lease of the Pittsburg, Fort Wayne and Chicago Railway, and was not turned over by the Pennsylvania Railroad to the Pennsylvania Company at the time the other property representing that lease was transferred. This bonus stock never cost us a dollar, and places the entire line within our control.

The five thousand eight hundred and two shares of preferred stock were received for moneys advanced for equipment and the extension of the line from Millersburg to Columbus. With the completion of a branch of this road down to Dresden Junction, it will, in addition to developing the coal on its main line and this branch, form a direct connection with the great coal fields of the Hocking Valley and the Cincinnati and Muskingum road. Therefore, our President has no doubt whatever that it will be amply able to take care of all its interest and pay a dividend on its preferred stock.

PITTSBURG, CINCINNATI AND ST. LOUIS RAILWAY.		Par Value.	Total Par Value.	Assessed Value.	Total Assessed Value.
Common stock,	$2,508,300 00				
Preferred first stock,	2,925,450 00				
Preferred second stock,	3,000,000 00				
First mortgage consolidated bonds,	6,222,000 00				
Second mortgage consolidated bonds,	5,000,000 00				
First mortgage Steubenville and Indiana Railroad (re-organized),	3,000,000 00				
Other bonds,	781,560 99				
	$23,437,310 99				
Floating debt,	3,854,872 55				
Total,	$27,292,183 54				
Operations for year—					
Net earnings Pittsburg, Cincinnati and St. Louis Railway,	$426,686 56				
Net earnings leased roads,	418,294 25				
Total,	$844,980 81				
Rent paid leased roads,	$2,089,111 99				
Rent paid Steubenville bridge,	100,000 00				
Amount required to pay interest on its bonded debt,	721,404 47				
Total,	$2,910,516 46				
Less net earnings,	844,980 81				
Deficit for year,	$2,065,535 65				

The leased roads on which the above loss occurs are leased to the Pittsburg, Cincinnati and St. Louis Railway Company at a stipulated rent, the Pennsylvania Railroad Company being the guarantor. The agreement of the Pennsylvania Railroad Company with the Pennsylvania Company requires that the Pennsylvania Company takes the place of the Pennsylvania Railway Company as guarantor. Hence, all the means of the Pittsburg, Cincinnati and St. Louis Railway Company are required to be exhausted before the Pennsylvania Company can be called on. Thus, these losses were liquidated by placing an additional mortgage on the Pittsburg, Cincinnati and St. Louis Railway, which mortgage was purchased by the Pennsylvania Company, and the proceeds used by the Pittsburg, Cincinnati and St. Louis Railway Company.

Held by Pennsylvania Railroad Company:					
Consolidated mortgage bonds,		. . .	$1,029,000	. . .	$668,850
Steubenville and Indiana seven per cent. bonds,		. . .	278,000	. . .	208,500
Second preferred stock Pittsburg, Cincinnati and St. Louis Railway,		. . .	3,000,000	. . .	. . . . .

CHARTIERS RAILWAY.		Par Value.	Total Par Value.	Assessed Value.	Total Assessed Value.
Leased to Pittsburg, Cincinnati and St. Louis Railway Company at cost; minimum, $35,000.					
Capital stock,	$800,000 00				
First mortgage bonds, seven per cent.,	500,000 00				
Held by Pennsylvania Railroad Company:					
Capital stock,	$325,000 00	$50	$325,000		
Net income for 1873, (sufficient to pay interest,)	35,000 00				

The officers of the Pennsylvania Railroad Company make the following report on the stock:—This stock was subscribed with the view of enabling the people living on the line between Mansfield and Washington, Pa., to form connections with the Pittsburg, Cincinnati and St. Louis Railway at the town of Mansfield. The road is twelve miles long, and runs over nine miles of the Pittsburg, Cincinnati and St. Louis line into Pittsburg, forming a line thirty-one miles long between Pittsburg and Washington. It has been leased to the Pittsburg, Cincinnati and St. Louis Railway, to be worked at cost, for the benefit of its bond and share holders, the Pennsylvania Railroad Company holding a majority of its shares. The operations of the line are demonstrating its ability to meet the interest on its mortgage bonds, and as the large coal deposits on the line are developed it may, within a very few years, be able to make some dividend upon its stock.

LITTLE MIAMI RAILROAD.		Par Value.	Total Par Value.	Assessed Value.	Total Assessed Value.
Leased to Pittsburg, Cincinnati and St. Louis Railway Company, the Pennsylvania Railroad Company guarantor, and the Pennsylvania Company sub-tenant, assuming the place of guarantor.					
Rent, 1873, (a sum sufficient to pay interest on its funded debt and eight per cent. dividend on its capital stock,)	$710,769 00				
Held by Pennsylvania Railroad Company:					
Capital stock, (eight per cent.,)	$281,200 00	$50	$281,200	. . .	$281,200

HOLLIDAY'S COVE RAILROAD.					
Held by Pennsylvania Railroad Company:					
	$20,000 00	$1,000	$20,000	. . .	$20,000
Redeemed since January 1st, 1874, at par.					

CINCIN'TI AND MUSKINGUM VALLEY R.W.					
Capital stock,	$3,996,610 00				
First mortgage bonds, seven per cent.,	1,500,000 00				
Held by Pennsylvania Railroad Company:					
First mortgage bonds, seven per cent.,	$752,000 00	$1,000	$752,000	. . .	$526,400
Net earnings for 1873,	19,429 00				
This road earned, 1872, (net,)	135,714 00				

These bonds were taken to represent the interest this Company held in that line, to aid in its extension from Zanesville to Dresden. It now forms connection with the Pittsburg, Cincinnati and St. Louis Railway through to Cincinnati, via Morrow, and forms an outlet for the Hocking Valley coal,—a traffic which promises to be of great value to this Company in the near future.

NEWPORT AND CINCINNATI BRIDGE.		Par Value.	Total Par Value.	Assessed Value.	Total Assessed Value.
Capital stock,	$1,200,000 00				
Bonded debts, seven per cent.,	1,200,000 00				
Floating debts,	812,766 55				
Held by Pennsylvania Railroad Company:					
Capital stock,	$720,000 00	$100	$720,000	. . .	$108,000
First mortgage bonds, seven per cent.,	1,200,000 00	1,000	1,200,000	. . .	1,020,000
Net earnings for 1873,	53,109 00				

The following is the report received from the officers of the Pennsylvania Railroad in relation to this property:—This stock was received by this Company as a bonus on the purchase of the bonds for the construction of the bridge across the Ohio, at Cincinnati. The $1,200,000 of first mortgage bonds were taken by this Company under an agreement by which this stock was given us, which, being sixty per cent. of the entire amount, gives us the control of the river at that point, with practically no cost whatever. The railroad companies south of the river and to Cincinnati, at the time this bridge was projected, came under a guaranty of $75,000 per annum for the railway traffic alone, the incidental traffic to belong to the Company. The business is being developed, and promises satisfactory results.

COLUMBUS, CHICAGO AND INDIANA CENTRAL RAILWAY.		Par Value.	Total Par Value.	Assessed Value.	Total Assessed Value.
This road is leased to the Pittsburg, Cincinnati and St. Louis Railway Company at thirty per cent. of its gross receipts, the minimum rental being seven per cent. on $15,821,000, being its entire indebtedness at the time of execution of lease. The Pennsylvania Railroad Company guarantees the fulfillment of the contract on the part of the Pittsburg, Cincinnati and St. Louis Railway Company.					
Capital stock, common,	$13,328,560 00				
Funded debt—					
First and second mortgage bonds,	15,344,750 00				
First and second mortgage bonds,	1,831,900 00				
Income,	3,747,000 00				
Income, convertible,	2,554,000 00				
Income,	74,024 25				
Total,	$23,551,674 25				
Gross receipts,	$4,477,806 84				
Thirty per cent. being	1,343,342 00				
It will be seen by this statement that the rental was nearly sufficient to pay interest on its first and second mortgage bonds.					
Held by Pennsylvania Railroad Company:					
Second mortgage bonds,	$1,258,000 00	. . .	$1,258,000	. . .	$880,600
Income,	3,504,000 00	. . .	3,504,000	. . .	1,752,000

	Par Value.	Total Par Value.	Assessed Value.	Total Assessed Value.
ST. LOUIS, VANDALIA AND TERRE HAUTE RAILROAD.				
Leased to Terre Haute and Indianapolis Railroad Company, and by them to Pennsylvania Company, &c., at its full net earnings, minimum rent to be thirty per cent. of its gross receipts.				
Bonded debt—				
First mortgage bonds, seven per cent., . . . $1,899,000 00				
Second mortgage bonds, seven per cent., . . . 2,600,000 00				
Income bonds, seven per cent., ... 1,000,000 00				
$5,499,000 00				
Floating debt—				
Rent received, ... $354,762 00				
Interest on bonds and taxes, ... 342,193 00				
Applicable to interest on income bonds, . . . $12,569 00				
Held by Pennsylvania Railroad Company:				
Second mortgage bonds, seven per cent., . . . $225,000 00	$1,000	$225,000	. . .	$157,500
Income bonds, seven per cent., ... 700,000 00	1,000	700,000	. . .	350,000
It would require an increase in gross receipts of only $200,000 to enable this Company to pay interest on its entire indebtedness.				
SHAMOKIN COAL COMPANY.				
Capital stock, ... $1,000,000 00				
First mortgage bonds, seven per cent., . . 100,000 00				
Floating debt, ... 122,246 28				
Held by Pennsylvania Railroad Company:				
Capital stock, ... $981,575 00	$25	$981,575	. . .	$392,630

LYKENS VALLEY COAL COMPANY.	Par Value.	Total Par Value.	Assessed Value.	Total Assessed Value.
Capital stock, ... $494,150 00				
Bonded debt, ... 106,000 00				
Held by Pennsylvania Railroad Company:				
Capital stock, ... $302,000 00	$50	$302,000	. . .	$395,765
Loss for 1873, ... 285,071 57				

This stock cost the Pennsylvania Railroad Company $395,765, and is abundantly worth its cost. The loss for 1873 is more apparent than real,—the outlay having been made for the erection of new breakers and general improvements. For further particulars, see report on coal properties.

SUMMIT BRANCH RAILROAD.	Par Value.	Total Par Value.	Assessed Value.	Total Assessed Value.
Capital stock, ... $3,828,100 00				
Bonded debt, ... 715,000 00				
Floating debt, ... 33,959 82				
Held by Pennsylvania Railroad Company:				
Capital stock, ... $1,252,400 00	$50	$1,252,400	. . .	$1,127,160
Net earnings for 1873, (equal to a dividend of eight and three-quarters per cent.,) . 348,368 97				

For further particulars, see report on coal properties.

SUSQUEHANNA COAL COMPANY.	Par Value.	Total Par Value.	Assessed Value.	Total Assessed Value.
Capital stock, ... $1,500,000 00				
Bonded debt, ... 1,783,000 00				
Floating debt, ... 854,790 70				
Held by Pennsylvania Railroad Company:				
Capital stock, ... $1,000,000 00	$100	$1,000,000	. . .	$1,000,000
Net earnings for 1873, (equal to a dividend of fourteen per cent.,) . 319,932 32				

This stock represents the entire coal field controlled by that company near Wilkesbarre, Pa., which is growing into great value.

APPENDIX B.

Comparative Statement of Earnings and Expenses of Leased Lines of Pennsylvania Company (including Indianapolis and Vincennes Railroad) for six months ending June 30th, 1874, and June 30th, 1873.

PITTSBURG, FT. WAYNE AND CHICAGO RAILWAY.

	Gross Earnings.	Expenses.	Net Earnings.
For six months ending June 30th, 1874	$4,474,158 73	$2,684,826 67	$1,789,332 06
Same period last year, ...	5,084,140 84	3,116,137 89	1,968,002 95
Increase, ...	. . . . . .	. . . . . .	. . . . . .
Decrease, ...	$609,982 11	$431,311 22	$178,670 89

ERIE AND PITTSBURG RAILROAD.

	Gross Earnings.	Expenses.	Net Earnings.
For six months ending June 30th, 1874	$440,619 84	$231,554 36	$209,065 48
Same period last year, ...	601,874 53	338,317 18	263,557 35
Increase, ...	. . . . . .	. . . . . .	. . . . . .
Decrease, ...	$161,254 69	$106,762 82	$54,491 87

CLEVELAND AND PITTSBURG RAILROAD.

	Gross Earnings.	Expenses.	Net Earnings.
For six months ending June 30th, 1874	$1,460,387 03	$710,755 79	$749,631 24
Same period last year, ...	1,790,470 67	951,833 14	838,637 53
Increase, ...	. . . . . .	. . . . . .	. . . . . .
Decrease, ...	$330,083 64	$241,077 35	$89,006 29

Indianapolis and Vincennes Railroad.

	Gross Earnings.	Expenses.	Net Earnings.
For six months ending June 30th, 1874	$126,922 69	$99,463 40	$27,459 29
Same period last year, ...	118,983 45	97,993 19	20,990 26
Increase, ...	$7,939 24	$1,470 21	$6,469 03
Decrease, ...			

Jeffersonville, Madison and Indianapolis Railroad.

	Gross Earnings.	Expenses.	Net Earnings.
For six months ending June 30th, 1874	$593,565 34	$413,005 84	$180,559 50
Same period last year, ...	641,660 10	483,715 98	157,944 12
Increase, ...			$22,615 38
Decrease, ...	$48,094 76	$70,710 14	

Comparative Statement of Earnings of Pennsylvania Company, from other sources than Leased Lines, for six months ending June 30th, 1874, and June 30th, 1873.

	Interest on Bonds and Dividends on Stock.	Earnings of the Monongahela Extension.	Car Equipment, &c.	Total.
For six months ending June 30th, 1874,	$542,265 60	$7,431 34	$722,377 69	$1,272,074 63
Same period 1873, .	113,879 18	5,557 94	146,451 77	265,888 89
Increase, ...	$428,386 42	$1,873 40	$575,925 92	$1,006,185 74
Decrease, . . .				

Recapitulation for six months ending June 30th, 1874.

Net earnings—leased lines and Indianapolis and Vincennes Railroad, ...	$2,956,047 57
Net earnings—car equipment, interest, dividends, &c., ...	1,272,074 63
Aggregate, ...	$4,228,122 20
Same period last year, ...	3,515,021 10
Increase, ...	$713,101 10

Comparative Statement of Earnings and Expenses of Leased Lines, and of Pittsburg, Cincinnati and St. Louis Railway Company, for six months ending June 30th, 1874, and June 30th, 1873.

PITTSBURG, CINCINNATI AND ST. LOUIS RAILWAY.

	Gross Earnings.	Expenses.	Net Earnings.
For six months ending June 30th, 1874	$1,785,021 24	$1,275,977 82	$509,043 42
Same period of last year,	1,900,057 11	1,559,179 97	340,877 14
Increase,			$168,166 28
Decrease,	$115,035 87	$283,202 15	

CHARTIERS RAILWAY.

	Gross Earnings.	Expenses.	Net Earnings.
For six months ending June 30th, 1874	$32,913 80	$20,723 42	$12,190 38
Same period of last year,	26,188 14	19,961 13	6,227 01
Increase,	$6,725 66	$762 29	$5,963 37
Decrease,			

COLUMBUS, CHICAGO AND INDIANA CENTRAL RAILWAY.

	Gross Earnings.	Expenses.	Net Earnings.
For six months ending June 30th, 1874	$1,931,458 55	$1,491,640 37	$439,818 18
Same period of last year,	2,281,535 91	2,000,615 12	280,920 79
Increase,			$158,897 39
Decrease,	$350,077 36	$508,974 75	

CINCINNATI AND MUSKINGUM VALLEY RAILWAY.

	Gross Earnings.	Expenses.	Net Earnings.
For six months ending June 30th, 1874	$183,560 37	$212,629 29	$29,068 92 *Expenses over earnings.*
Same period of last year,	215,644 42	200,537 68	15,106 74
Increase,		$12,091 61	
Decrease,	$32,084 05		$44,175 66

Little Miami Railroad.

	Gross Earnings.	Expenses.	Net Earnings.
For six months ending June 30th, 1874	$588,176 95	$497,499 49	$90,677 46
Same period of last year, ...	655,081 45	618,981 64	36,099 81
Increase, ...	. . . . . .	. . . . . .	$54,577 65
Decrease, ...	$66,904 50	$121,482 15	. . . . . .

Recapitulation.

Net earnings, all the lines, for six months ending June 30th, 1874, . $1,022,660 52
"   "   "   same period last year, ...   679,231 49

Increase, ... $343,429 03

APPENDIX C.

Comparative Statement of Earnings and Expenses of Pennsylvania Railroad and Branches, and United Railroads of New Jersey, for the first six months of 1873 and 1874.

PENNSYLVANIA RAILROAD—MAIN LINE.

	Earnings.	Expenses.	Net Earnings.
January 1st to July 1st, 1874,	$9,930,362 52	$5,600,784 98	$4,329,577 54
Same period of 1873,	11,175,321 58	7,280,026 70	3,895,294 88
Increase,			$434,282 66
Decrease,	$1,244,959 06	$1,679,241 72	

PENNSYLVANIA RAILROAD—BRANCHES.

	Earnings.	Expenses.	Net Earnings.
January 1st to July 1st, 1874,	$1,192,666 48	$906,336 36	$286,330 12
Same period of 1873,	1,203,006 21	1,021,114 32	181,891 89
Increase,			$104,438 23
Decrease,	$10,339 73	$114,777 96	

UNITED RAILROADS OF NEW JERSEY.

	Earnings.	Expenses.	Net Earnings.
January 1st to July 1st, 1874,	$4,276,040 05	$3,128,982 31	$1,147,057 74
Same period of 1873,	4,133,816 46	3,617,150 07	516,666 39
Increase,	$142,223 59		$630,391 35
Decrease,		$488,167 76	

The total amount of rentals * paid branch roads (and not included in expenses of branch roads) for six months of 1873 was $189,588.25, and for same period of 1874 was $219,142.43.

---
* Rentals are net earnings paid branches.

APPENDIX D.

Statement of Gross Earnings, Number of Tons of Freight Moved, and Number of Passengers Carried on the Lines of Railway Operated or otherwise Controlled by Pennsylvania Company for the year 1873, as compared with 1868.

PITTSBURG, FORT WAYNE AND CHICAGO RAILWAY.

Earnings.	1873.	1868.	Increase.	Decrease.	Remarks.
Freight,	$6,716,398 88	$5,231,857 73	$1,484,541 15		
Passenger,	2,459,074 11	2,492,265 46		$33,191 35	
Miscellaneous,	443,601 37	317,957 51	126,543 86		
Total,	$9,619,074 36	$8,041,180 70	$1,577,893 66		
Tons of freight,	2,292,644	1,509,052	783,592		
Passengers carried,	2,132,585	1,411,677	720,908		

NEW CASTLE AND BEAVER VALLEY RAILROAD.

Earnings.	1873.	1868.	Increase.	Decrease.	Remarks.
Freight,	$269,210 97	$145,985 81	$123,225 16		
Passenger,	77,247 01	63,915 17	13,331 84		
Miscellaneous,	4,631 50	7,762 70		$3,131 20	
Total,	$351,089 48	$217,663 68	$133,425 80		
Tons of freight,	648,488	351,773	296,715		
Passengers carried,	172,638	143,435	29,203		

LAWRENCE RAILROAD.

Earnings.	1873.	1868.	Increase.	Decrease.	Remarks.
Freight,	$155,440 80	$77,329 98	$78,110 82		
Passenger,	29,621 58	24,643 32	4,978 26		
Miscellaneous,	4,320 00	4,180 00	140 00		
Total,	$189,382 38	$106,153 30	$83,229 08		
Tons of freight,	337,757	167,683	170,074		
Passengers carried,	77,923	66,829	11,094		

ERIE AND PITTSBURG RAILROAD.

Earnings.	1873.	1868.	Increase.	Decrease.	Remarks.
Freight,	$888,135 69	$512,291 68	$375,844 01		
Passenger,	163,097 55	124,890 41	38,207 14		
Miscellaneous,	114,059 38	19,925 61	94,133 77		
Total,	$1,165,292 62	$657,107 70	$508,184 92		
Tons of freight,	1,033,789	456,713	577,076		
Passengers carried,	266,755	147,146	119,609		

CLEVELAND AND PITTSBURG RAILROAD.

Earnings.	1873.	1868.	Increase.	Decrease.	Remarks.
Freight,	$2,905,769 49	$1,625,297 30	$1,280,472 19		
Passenger,	659,705 12	611,970 37	47,734 75		
Miscellaneous,	106,260 64	82,865 19	23,395 45		
Total,	$3,671,735 25	$2,320,132 86	$1,351,602 39		
Tons of freight,	1,907,484	1,005,773	901,711		
Passengers carried,	628,956	617,602	11,354		

JEFFERSONVILLE, MADISON AND INDIANAPOLIS RAILROAD.

Earnings.	1873.	1868.	Increase.	Decrease.	Remarks.
Freight,	$908,886 08	$552,596 18	$356,289 90		NOTE.—The large increase in number of passengers carried, in the face of a diminution in passenger earnings, is due to the establishment of the hourly line between Louisville and Jeffersonville and New Albany. These passengers average over one thousand per day, and pay a little over eight cents each.
Passenger,	376,294 07	434,546 65		$58,252 58	
Miscellaneous,	83,939 80	76,380 90	7,558 90		
Total,	*$1,369,119 95	$1,063,523 73	$305,596 22		
Tons of freight,	624,102	264,669	359,433		
Passengers carried,	658,928	317,929	340,999		

*These earnings are those of the Jeffersonville, Madison and Indianapolis Road proper, excluding the Shelby and Rush Railroad and Cambridge Extension. The Pennsylvania Company's proportion of earnings of latter in 1873 was $65,873.06.

INDIANAPOLIS AND VINCENNES RAILROAD.

Earnings.	1873.	1871.	Increase.	Decrease.	Remarks.
Freight,	$146,189 05	$153,684 11		$7,495 06	
Passenger,	95,256 21	88,209 83	$7,046 38		
Miscellaneous,	12,338 88	13,393 99		1,055 11	
Total,	$253,784 14	$255,287 93		$1,503 79	
Tons of freight,	77,483	81,314 Estimated.		3,831	
Passengers carried,	113,616	105,012 Estimated.	8,604		

INDIANAPOLIS AND ST. LOUIS RAILROAD.

Earnings.	1873.	1871.	Increase.	Decrease.	Remarks.
Freight,	$586,027 60	$496,491 42	$89,536 18		
Passenger,	120,933 98	143,304 72		$22,370 74	
Miscellaneous,	21,914 31	31,760 58		9,846 27	
Total,	$728,875 89	$671,556 72	$57,319 17		
Tons of freight,	553,069	411,849	141,220		
Passengers carried,	95,650	94,223	1,427		

St. Louis, Alton and Terre Haute Railroad.

Earnings.	1873.	1868.	Increase.	Decrease.	Remarks.
Freight,	$973,903 81	$947,055 82	$26,847 99		
Passenger,	296,515 72	676,120 56		$379,604 84	
Miscellaneous,	98,233 04	106,897 95		8,664 91	
Total,	$1,368,652 57	$1,730,074 33		$361,421 76	
	1873.	1870.			
Tons of freight,	604,699	429,180	175,519		
Passengers carried,	247,327	301,318		53,991	

Little Miami Railroad.

Earnings.	1873.	1868.	Increase.	Decrease.	Remarks.
Freight,	$697,573 52	$847,894 46		$150,320 94	
Passenger,	529,489 17	754,360 00		224,870 83	
Miscellaneous,	144,485 13	136,814 68	$7,670 45		
Total,	$1,371,547 82	$1,739,069 14		$367,521 32	
Tons of freight,	471,151	386,163 Estimated.	84,988		
Passengers carried,	723,785	707,311 Estimated.	16,474		

COLUMBUS, CHICAGO AND INDIANA CENTRAL RAILWAY.

Earnings.	1873.	1868.	Increase.	Decrease.	Remarks.
Freight,	$3,298,010 95	$1,993,206 64	$1,304,804 31		
Passenger,	995,797 77	1,025,096 02		$29,298 25	
Miscellaneous,	183,998 12	125,995 91	58,002 21		
Total,	$4,477,806 84	$3,144,298 57	$1,333,508 27		
Tons of freight,	1,473,623	810,243	663,380		
Passengers carried,	616,627	634,734		18,107	

ST. LOUIS, VANDALIA AND TERRE HAUTE RAILROAD.

Earnings.	1873.	1871.	Increase.	Decrease.	Remarks.
Freight,	$736,950 78	$666,167 39	$70,783 39		
Passenger,	331,207 91	361,695 24		$30,487 33	
Miscellaneous,	62,654 38	37,928 24	24,726 14		
Total,	$1,130,813 07	$1,065,790 87	$65,022 20		
Tons of freight,	478,188	394,181 Estimated.	84,007		
Passengers carried,	190,974	190,366 Estimated.	608		

Chartiers Railway.

Earnings.	1873.	1871.	Increase.	Decrease.	Remarks.
Freight,	$17,096 39	$16,626 57	$469 82		
Passenger,	41,938 81	30,275 23	11,663 58		
Miscellaneous,	2,523 42	6 93	2,516 49		
Total,	$61,558 62	$46,908 73	$14,649 89		
Tons of freight,	14,690	14,341 Estimated.	349		
Passengers carried,	107,209	77,629 Estimated.	29,580		

Pittsburg, Cincinnati and St. Louis Railway.

Earnings.	1873.	1868.	Increase.	Decrease.	Remarks.
Freight,	$2,725,024 37	$1,552,435 88	$1,172,588 49		
Passenger,	827,240 65	615,799 36	211,441 29		
Miscellaneous,	288,948 85	158,048 68	130,900 17		
Total,	$3,841,213 87	$2,326,283 92	$1,514,929 95		
Tons of freight,	1,472,709	617,364 Estimated.	855,345		
Passengers carried,	652,898	439,857 Estimated.	213,041		

230

Cincinnati and Muskingum Valley Railway.

Earnings.	1873.	1868.	Increase.	Decrease.	Remarks.
Freight,	$301,257 05	$203,808 60	$97,448 45		Length of road in 1873, 148 4/10 miles. Length of road in 1868, 132 7/8 miles.
Passenger,	124,228 41	109,406 93	14,821 48		
Miscellaneous,	17,731 22	33,554 44		$15,823 22	
Total,	$443,216 68	$346,769 97	$96,446 71		
Tons of freight,	166,177	91,121 Estimated.	75,056		
Passengers carried,	145,089	108,265 Estimated.	36,824		

APPENDIX E.

Statement of Bonds of the several companies with time of maturity, in chronological order.

EAST OF PITTSBURG.

When due.			
Overdue.	New Jersey Railroad and Transportation Company,	$100,000 00	
Ninety days after demand.	United Companies,	500,000 00	
Overdue, 1873.	East Brandywine and Waynesburg Railroad,	35,000 00	$635,000 00
1874.	Pennsylvania Railroad Company, for main line,	$460,000 00	460,000 00
1875.	Pennsylvania Railroad Company second mortgage,	$4,865,000 00	
1875.	Pennsylvania Railroad Company, for main line,	460,000 00	
1875.	United Companies—Joint Companies,	675,000 00	
1875.	United Companies—New Jersey Railroad and Transportation Company,	300,000 00	
1875.	Allegheny Valley Railroad first mortgage,	37,000 00	6,337,000 00
1876.	Pennsylvania Railroad Company, for main line,	$460,000 00	460,000 00
1877.	Pennsylvania Railroad Company, for main line,	$460,000 00	
1877.	Philadelphia and Erie Railroad—Sunbury and Lewistown,	1,000,000 00	
1877.	Belvidere Delaware Railroad first mortgage,	1,000,000 00	
1877.	Northern Central Railway third mortgage,	500,000 00	2,960,000 00

1878.	Pennsylvania Railroad Company, for main line,	$460,000 00	
1878.	United Companies—New Jersey Railroad and Transportation Company,	450,000 00	$910,000 00
1879.	Pennsylvania Railroad Company, for main line,	$460,000 00	460,000 00
1880.	Pennsylvania Railroad Company, for main line,	$460,000 00	
1880.	Pennsylvania Railroad Company first mortgage,	4,970,000 00	
1880.	United Companies—Joint Companies,	1,310,000 00	
1880.	Northern Central Railway income bonds,	1,000,000 00	
1880.	Elmira and Williamsport Railroad first mortgage,	1,000,000 00	8,740,000 00
1881.	Pennsylvania Railroad Company, for main line,	$460,000 00	
1881.	Bald Eagle Valley Railroad first mortgage,	345,900 00	
1881.	Ebensburg and Cresson Railroad first mortgage,	80,000 00	
1881.	Philadelphia and Erie Railroad first mortgage whole line,	5,000,000 00	5,885,900 00
1882.	Pennsylvania Railroad Company, for main line,	$460,000 00	
1882.	Junction Railroad Company first mortgage,	500,000 00	
1882.	Oil Creek Railroad—Warren and Franklin,	580,000 00	1,540,000 00
1883.	Pennsylvania Railroad Company, for main line,	$460,000 00	
1883.	United Companies—Joint Companies,	1,700,000 00	2,160,000 00
1884.	Pennsylvania Railroad Company, for main line,	$460,000 00	
1884.	Bald Eagle Valley Railroad second mortgage,	100,000 00	
1884.	Cumberland Valley Railroad common,	81,800 00	641,800 00

Statement of Bonds, with time of maturity, in chronological order.

EAST OF PITTSBURG.—*Continued.*

When due.			
1885.	Pennsylvania Railroad Company, for main line,	$460,000 00	
1885.	East Brandywine and Waynesburg Railroad first mortgage,	140,000 00	
1885.	Danville, Hazleton and Wilkesbarre Railroad second mortgage,	300,000 00	
1885.	Belvidere Delaware Railroad second mortgage,	499,500 00	
1885.	Northern Central Railway second mortgage,	2,500,000 00	$3,899,500 00
1887.	Danville, Hazleton and Wilkesbarre Railroad first mortgage,	$1,400,000 00	
1887.	Belvidere Delaware Railroad third mortgage,	745,000 00	
1887.	Pennsylvania Canal,	90,000 00	2,235,000 00
1888.	Philadelphia and Erie Railroad second mortgage,	$3,000,000 00	
1888.	United Railroad Companies,	154,000 00	
1888.	Oil Creek Railroad consolidated,	1,100,000 00	4,254,000 00
1889.	United Railroad Companies—Joint Companies,	$866,000 00	
1889.	United Railroad Companies mortgage bonds,	5,000,000 00	
1889.	Pemberton and Hightstown Railroad,	160,000 00	6,026,000 00
1890.	Sunbury and Lewistown Railroad first mortgage,	$1,200,000 00	
1890.	Oil Creek Railroad first mortgage,	500,000 00	1,700,000 00

235

1891.	Sunbury and Lewistown Railroad income,	$200,000 00	$200,000 00
1892.	Bedford and Bridgeport Railroad first mortgage,	$1,000,000 00	1,000,000 00
1893.	Western Pennsylvania Railroad first mortgage main line,	$800,000 00	
1893.	Allegheny Valley Railroad second mortgage,	8,000 00	808,000 00
1894.	United Railroad Companies,	$1,846,000 00	
1894.	United Railroad Companies,	1,800,000 00	
1894.	United Railroad Companies,	2,000,000 00	5,646,000 00
1896.	Western Pennsylvania Railroad, Pittsburg Branch,	$1,000,000 00	
1896.	Allegheny Valley Railroad general mortgage,	3,934,000 00	
1896.	Oil Creek Railroad—O. C. first mortgage,	1,500,000 00	6,434,000 00
1897.	Mifflin and Centre County Railroad,	$200,000 00	
1897.	Camden and Burlington County Railroad,	350,000 00	
1898.	East Brandywine and Waynesburg Railroad—N. H. Extension,	50,000 00	
1899.	Mount Holly, Lumberton and Medford Railroad,	75,000 00	675,000 00
1900.	Junction Railroad, (Philadelphia,)	$300,000 00	
1900.	Connecting Railroad, (Philadelphia,) first series,	200,000 00	
1900.	Northern Central Railway third mortgage,	1,223,000 00	
1900.	Northern Central Railway consolidated,	2,520,000 00	
1900.	Northern Central Railway consolidated registered,	205,000 00	4,448,000 00

Statement of Bonds, with time of maturity, in chronological order.

EAST OF PITTSBURG.—*Continued.*

When due.			
1901.	Western Pennsylvania Railroad general mortgage,	$1,200,000 00	
1901.	United Railroad Companies,	3,000,000 00	
1901.	Connecting Railroad second series,	200,000 00	
1901.	Shamokin Valley and Pottsville Railroad,	1,994,000 00	$6,394,000 00
1902.	Lewisburg, Centre and Spruce Creek Railroad,	$1,545,000 00	
1902.	Connecting Railroad third series,	200,000 00	1,745,000 00
1903.	Pennsylvania and Delaware Railroad first mortgage,	$1,083,000 00	
1903.	Pennsylvania and Delaware Railroad second mortgage,	519,000 00	
1903.	Connecting Railroad fourth series,	200,000 00	1,802,000 00
1904.	Cumberland Valley Railroad first mortgage,	$161,000 00	
1904.	Connecting Railroad fifth series,	200,000 00	361,000 00
1905.	Pennsylvania Railroad Company consolidated,	$8,245,000 00	8,245,000 00
1908.	Cumberland Valley Railroad second mortgage,	$109,500 00	109,500 00
1910.	Pennsylvania Railroad Company general,	$19,558,760 00	
1910.	Pennsylvania Canal general,	2,551,000 00	22,109,760 00

237

1911.	Baltimore and Potomac Railroad main line,	$3,000,000 00	
1911.	Baltimore and Potomac Railroad tunnel,	1,500,000 00	$4,500,000 00
1920.	Philadelphia and Erie Railroad third mortgage, gold,	$5,730,000 00	5,730,000 00
1922.	Northern Central Railway income,	$3,000,000 00	3,000,000 00
Irredeemable.	Northern Central Railway—Maryland State loan,	$1,500,000 00	1,500,000 00
Not stated.	Elmira and Williamsport Railroad mortgage on real estate,	$50,000 00	50,000 00
2862.	Elmira and Williamsport Railroad income bonds,	$570,000 00	570,000 00

WEST OF PITTSBURG.

When due.			
1874.	Pittsburg, Fort Wayne and Chicago Railway equipment bonds,	$1,000,000 00	$1,000,000 00
1875.	Cleveland and Pittsburg Railroad third mortgage,	$1,252,000 00	1,252,000 00
1876.	Pittsburg, Fort Wayne and Chicago Railway—Ohio and Pittsburg bridge,	$44,000 00	44,000 00
1880.	Little Miami Railroad—Cincinnati loan,	$100,000 00	100,000 00
1881.	Indianapolis and St. Louis Railroad equipment bonds,	$378,000 00	
1881.	Jeffersonville, Madison and Indianapolis Railroad—Indianapolis and Madison,	399,000 00	777,000 00

Statement of Bonds, with time of maturity, in chronological order.

WEST OF PITTSBURG.—*Continued.*

When due.			
1882.	Erie and Pittsburg Railroad first mortgage,	$292,200 00	
1882.	Columbus, Chicago and Indiana Central Railway second mortgage—Indiana Central,	666,500 00	$958,700 00
1883.	Little Miami Railroad,	$1,490,000 00	
1883.	Columbus, Chicago and Indiana Central Railway (Col. and Ind.) preferred,	157,000 00	
1883.	Columbus, Chicago and Indiana Central Railway (Col. and Ind.) common,	152,500 00	
1883.	Columbus, Chicago and Indiana Central Railway (Col. and Ind.) second mortgage,	3,500 00	1,803,000 00
1884.	Pittsburg, Cincinnati and St. Louis Railway (Springfield and Illinois) first mortgage,	$3,000,000 00	
1884.	Columbus, Chicago and Indiana Central Railway (T. L. and B.) first mortgage,	554,500 00	3,554,500 00
1886.	Columbus, Chicago and Indiana Central Railway (Cin. and Chic. Air-Line) first mort.	$39,650 00	39,650 00
1887.	Pittsburg, Fort Wayne and Chicago Railway consolidated,	$100,000 00	100,000 00
1890.	Erie and Pittsburg Railroad second mortgage,	$92,800 00	
1890.	Pittsburg, Cincinnati and St. Louis Railway consolidated,	6,222,000 00	
1890.	Pittsburg, Cincinnati and St. Louis Railway (S. and I.) consolidated, Newark Division,	775,000 00	
1890.	Little Miami Railroad—Col. and Xenia,	302,000 00	
1890.	Columbus, Chicago and Indiana Central Railway—Cin. and Chic. Air-Line,	194,100 00	
1890.	Columbus, Chicago and Indiana Central Railway second mortgage,	3,747,000 00	11,332,900 00
1892.	Cleveland and Pittsburg Railroad fourth mortgage,	$1,096,000 00	1,096,000 00

1893.	Columbus, Chicago and Indiana Central Railway (C. and G. E.) first mortgage,	$220,000 00	$220,000 00
1895.	Little Miami Railroad—D. and W.,	$463,000 00	
1895.	Little Miami Railroad (D. and W.) old,	189,000 00	
1895.	Columbus, Chicago and Indiana Central Railway (C. and G. E.) last,	241,000 00	893,000 00
1897.	St. Louis, Vandalia and Terre Haute first mortgage,	$1,900,000 00	1,900,000 00
1898.	Erie and Pittsburg Railroad consolidated,	$2,192,000 00	
1898.	St. Louis, Vandalia and Terre Haute Railroad second mortgage,	2,600,000 00	4,792,000 00
1900.	Cleveland and Pittsburg Railroad, consolidated sinking fund,	$1,499,000 00	
1900.	Erie and Pittsburg Railroad equipment mortgage,	750,000 00	
1900.	Indianapolis and St. Louis Railroad second mortgage,	1,000,000 00	
1900.	Indianapolis and Vincennes Railroad second mortgage,	1,450,000 00	
1900.	Cleveland, Mount Vernon and Delaware Railroad first mortgage,	1,300,000 00	
1900.	Columbus, Chicago and Indiana Central Railway income convertible,	2,554,000 00	8,553,000 00
1901.	Ashtabula, Youngstown and Pittsburg Railroad first mortgage,	$1,500,000 00	
1901.	Chartiers Railway first mortgage,	500,000 00	
1901.	Cincinnati and Muskingum Valley Railway first mortgage,	1,500,000 00	
1901.	St. Louis, Vandalia and Terre Haute Railroad income,	1,000,000 00	4,500,000 00
1902.	Cleveland, Mount Vernon and Delaware Railroad second mortgage,	$1,000,000 00	1,000,000 00
1904.	Columbus, Chicago and Indiana Central Railway (C. and I. C.) first mortgage,	$2,638,000 00	
1904.	Columbus, Chicago and Indiana Central Railway (C. and I. C.) second mortgage,	821,000 00	3,459,000 00

Statement of Bonds, with time of maturity, in chronological order.

WEST OF PITTSBURG.—*Continued.*

When due.			
1905.	Columbus, Chicago and Indiana Central Railway—Union and Logansport Branch,	$815,000 00	$815,000 00
1906.	Jeffersonville, Madison and Indianapolis Railroad first mortgage,	$2,474,000 00	2,474,000 00
1908.	Indianapolis and Vincennes Railroad first mortgage,	$1,700,000 00	
1908.	Columbus, Chicago and Indiana Central Railway first mortgage consolidated,	10,333,000 00	12,033,000 00
1910.	Jeffersonville, Madison and Indianapolis Railroad second mortgage,	$2,000,000 00	2,000,000 00
1911.	Mansfield, Coldwater and Lake Michigan Railroad,	$4,460,000 00	4,460,000 00
1912.	Pittsburg, Fort Wayne and Chicago Railway first mortgage,	$5,250,000 00	
1912.	Pittsburg, Fort Wayne and Chicago Railway second mortgage,	5,160,000 00	
1912.	Pittsburg, Fort Wayne and Chicago Railway third mortgage,	2,000,000 00	12,410,000 00
1913.	Cleveland and Pittsburg Railroad construction and equipment,	$600,000 00	
1913.	Pittsburg, Cincinnati and St. Louis Railway second mortgage,	5,000,000 00	5,600,000 00
1919.	Indianapolis and St. Louis Railroad first mortgage,	$2,000,000 00	2,000,000 00
Not stated.	Columbus, Chicago and Indiana Central Railway—Ch. and G. E.,	$344,400 00	
Not stated.	Columbus, Chicago and Indiana Central Railway (T. L. and B.) income,	74,024 25	418,424 25

APPENDIX F.

Printed in Dunstable, United Kingdom